THE EXQUISITE BOOK OF
PAPER FLOWER
TRANSFORMATIONS

**PLAYING WITH SIZE, SHAPE, AND COLOR TO CREATE
SPECTACULAR PAPER ARRANGEMENTS**

LIVIA CETTI

PHOTOGRAPHS BY KATE MATHIS

ABRAMS | NEW YORK

Editor: Cristina Garces
Designer: Jaspal Riyait
Production Manager: True Sims

Library of Congress Control Number: 2016943706

ISBN: 978-1-4197-2412-1

Printed and bound in the United States
10 9 8 7 6 5 4 3 2 1

Abrams books are available at special discounts when purchased in quantity
for premiums and promotions as well as fundraising or educational use.
Special editions can also be created to specification. For details, contact
specialsales@abramsbooks.com or the address below.

ABRAMS
The Art of Books

115 West 18th Street
New York, NY 10011
www.abramsbooks.com

CONTENTS

THE GEOMETRY OF NATURE

MY CREATIVE PROCESS, ESPECIALLY THAT OF MAKING PAPER FLOWERS, comes naturally to me, so putting it into words is always challenging. Reflecting on years of experience and practice, I can say that my sensibility is inspired largely by landscapes and nature and is greatly influenced by the same principles as *ikebana*, the art of Japanese flower arrangement. I know instinctively which shapes balance or offset form and have discovered how my intuition plays off of nature's own mathematical patterns.

When I set out to create a bloom or arrangement from an idea, a feeling, I turn to nature first. I try to see the flower in its most elemental state, and I take time to look at as many varieties of the actual flower as I can find. Then, I try to break the flower down into parts to further envision how the natural elements can be expressed by paper: petals, stamens, leaves, stems, sepals. For me this is very specific, even mathematical. Almost subconsciously, I create flowers that are, in their most simplified form, geometric shapes. Alliums are spheres or globes. Peegee hydrangeas are cones. Lilies of the valley are arcs. Tulips are bells. And my favorite arrangements always mix and match these shapes expertly to create a beautiful assortment of hard and soft edges. Every flower has its own geometry.

This book will teach you how to play with size, shape, color, and texture to create bright and exuberant paper flowers, each more lush and abundant than the last. Within, you will find instructions for creating bold, vibrant single stems in a variety of natural shapes: globes, spikes, bells, saucers, rectangles, cones, and arcs. By thinking of flowers as elemental shapes, it is easier to be free with your techniques and create blooms that are more natural looking and less manufactured. For example, the Hydrangea (page 46) is a complex repetition of a simple floret that is built out in a spherical form. The Cosmos (page 58) is a gorgeous saucer of a flower, with a face composed of repetitive petals that yearn for the sunlight. The Honeysuckle (page 108) is made up of little tubes that together make a fluid, dynamic vine that can be shaped and molded into a natural arc as you go.

Once you start to think of flowers as basic shapes, you can use that knowledge to build bigger, better arrangements. When I begin an arrangement, I like to play around with the blooms to create different effects. Tall spikes add drama, so I love beginning with Delphinium, Lupine, or Coleus. Large rectangles, like the Cyclamen and Bearded Iris, are eye-catching. Once I've built a foundation with larger shapes, I fill in the holes with medium and smaller shapes—the same pattern you might find looking at a landscape, where the tall trees dominate, the brush fills in the middle, and the pretty grasses complete the frame at the bottom. So I use the Hellebore (page 66) and Cornflower (page 54) to fill in medium spots. I like the simple Fluffy Poppy (page 42) for the smaller spaces.

Of course, you begin with shape, but color and texture are part of the picture, too. For arrangements featuring only one type of flower, playing around with color and texture adds another layer of interest. Here, I've also offered new techniques for painting, dyeing, and even constructing more architectural petals for creating a host of stunning and complex flowers. This unique visual approach allows for lots of creative experimentation, and the option for many, many personal variations of the flower instructions I offer here. I hope you'll see your own creative process take shape as you make your way through these wonderful projects and new techniques!

—LIVIA

9

GETTING STARTED

The projects in this book make use of some essential elements of paper flower making, which I'll explain in this chapter. For those of you who read my first book, *The Exquisite Book of Paper Flowers*, we'll revisit fundamentals such as cutting templates, taping wires, bleaching and coloring paper, and attaching petals, buds, leaves, and stems, and more. But you'll also find a host of new techniques, as the amazing flowers and projects in this book are a little bit more involved—more blooms, more petals, stronger stems, more complex final flowers. This is great news for you!

The most essential new techniques involve treating your tissue with new mediums. In addition to dipping tissue in bleach, I've found that simply using water creates a nicely subtle change in the texture of the tissue. And dipping tissue into fabric dye creates vivid two-tone, three-tone, sometimes even-more-tone options. For example, with dye, a bright pink strip can be made much more variegated, or you can choose to have several different colors all on one strip (see the Bearded Iris on page 78). The result is a wonderfully complex tissue effect, with the petals both more natural and more fanciful. Plus, not only can you mix your own colors, but the possibilities for color combinations are endless. And, if you need to make a perfect color match, you can achieve it with dye and customize your palette even more, giving you much more freedom to explore!

TOOLS

Over time, I've gotten comfortable with the tools I use. Here are the ones I use most often, and the ones you'll need to make the projects in this book.

1 | CUTTING MAT

Make sure your mat is at least 18" x 24" (46 x 61 cm).

2 | FRINGING SHEARS

Though not required to make the projects in this book, these are a good investment. They create a consistent fringe and save the time it would take to make individual fringe cuts.

3 | GLUE GUN

I prefer the high-heat type because when you attach leaves to the wire stem, the hotter glue creates a better bond, making the leaves less likely to snap off.

4 | MEDIUM KNIFE-EDGE SCISSORS

Used mostly for cutting tissue paper and Canson construction paper, they must be sharp to produce a clean edge. Use scissors with blades that aren't too long (they get in the way) and aren't too short (you won't be able to get a smooth cut). I like a 3" (7.5 cm) blade, as they are more comfortable to use and easier to control. It's important not to use fabric scissors when cutting paper—you'll ruin them.

5 | PAINTBRUSHES

I paint leaves and petal tissue, both individually and in bulk. When painting single leaves or petals, a soft brush with natural bristles is helpful for controlling the paint. When I'm painting a whole sheet of tissue or Canson paper, I like a medium soft brush, which takes more paint.

6 | QUILTING RULER

These clear acrylic rulers, marked with a grid, are used with a rotary cutter to cut all your tissue into manageable strips. I recommend a 6" x 24" (15 x 61 cm) ruler for optimal convenience.

7 | ROTARY CUTTER

This is an invaluable tool for cutting up to 12 layers of tissue paper at once.

8 | SCALLOPING SHEARS, DECKLED SHEARS, AND ZIGZAG SCISSORS

These specialty scissors are used for cutting petals with an unusual edge, such as the Narcissus (page 96), Delphinium (page 124), and Cornflower (page 54). Note: I sharpen these scissors by cutting into a small sheet of tinfoil a few times.

9 | WIRE CUTTERS

I like to use floral wire cutters, though wire cutters from a hardware store work just as well.

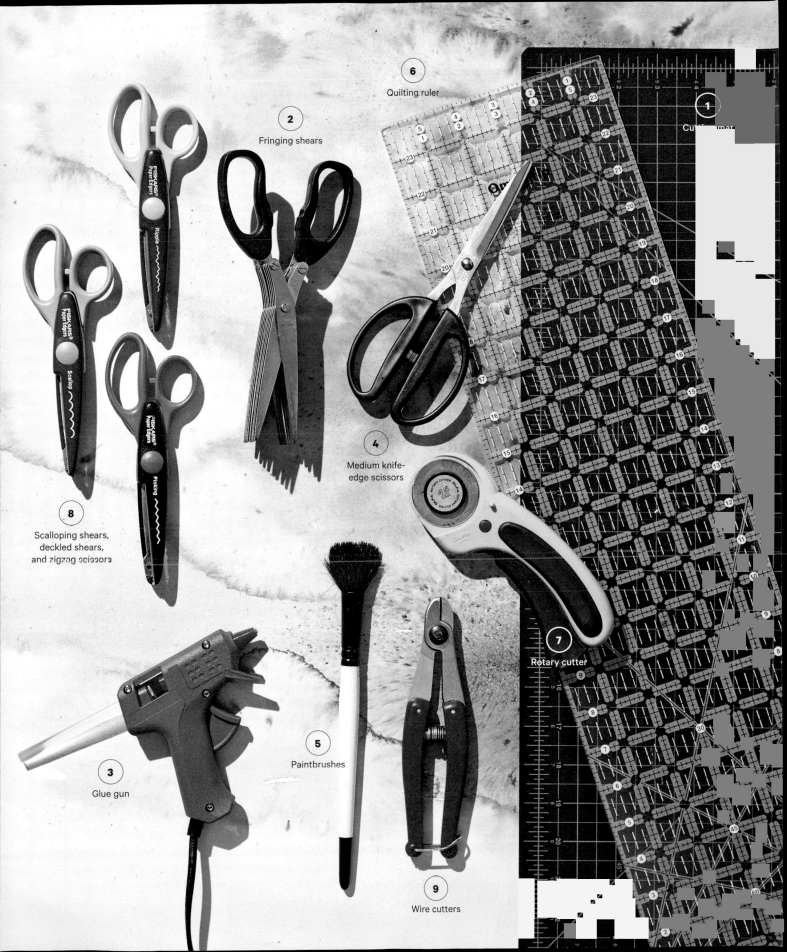

6 Quilting ruler

2 Fringing shears

1 Cutting mat

4 Medium knife-edge scissors

8 Scalloping shears, deckled shears, and zigzag scissors

7 Rotary cutter

3 Glue gun

5 Paintbrushes

9 Wire cutters

MATERIALS

Whether you buy online or at a craft store, finding the right materials is important. While I often purchase items in bulk so I have plenty on hand to play with, you may want to buy small amounts at first to discover which brands you like best. For tips on where to find specific items, check the Resources on page 173.

GENERAL MATERIALS

1 | DOUBLE-HEADED STAMENS

Premade new and vintage stamens come in bundles of fifty and are available in a variety of shapes and colors, including yellow, red, pink, lavender, and even black.

2 | FABRIC DYE

I use this dye to color petal tissue, primarily. I prefer Rit brand, but any widely available option will do. To use, mix half a packet of dye with 1 quart (960 ml) hot water, then stir with a paint stick to dissolve the pigment. I like to use old plastic takeout food containers to hold my dye, so that I always have a variety of colors ready to dye a lot of paper at once. If the dye begins to dry out, it can be reconstituted with hot water (it doesn't look as bright, but definitely works in a pinch).

3 | FLORAL TAPE

This paper-flower essential comes in an array of colors and in 1" (2.5 cm) and ½" (12 mm) widths. You'll need ½" (12 mm) tape in yellow, white, green, dark green, and gold for the projects in this book.

4 | FLORAL WIRE

You will need straight floral wire in 16-, 18-, 20-, 22-, and 24-gauge diameters. The standard wire length is 18" (46 cm), which you will cut down as needed to make the projects in the book.

5 | GOUACHE PAINT

I use this high-quality, opaque watercolor to paint centers, buds, petals, and leaves.

6 | HOT GLUE STICKS

I keep a supply on hand so I'm ready to plug in the glue gun and attach leaves to stems in an instant.

7 | MINI AND LARGE SAFETY COTTON SWABS

These are used for making the Poppy Center (see page 22) and elongated buds. Unlike a regular cotton swab, mini swabs (I like the ones by Muji) and safety swabs have a rounded center and a slightly pointed tip. Make sure the ones you buy have a hollow "stick."

STYROFOAM SHEETS

Not to be confused with the material used for disposable cups, this Styrofoam comes in white or green sheets. I use it for my potted plant arrangements.

WHITE CRAFTING GLUE

This adhesive is essential for working with delicate tissue and crepe paper and for applying glitter. It dries clear and is easy to use.

HOUSEHOLD BLEACH

Many of my tissue effects are created with a diluted bleach solution.

8
Canson paper
(see page 14)

2
Fabric dye

7
Mini and large safety
cotton swabs

3
Floral tape

6
Hot glue sticks

5
Gouache paint

1
Double-headed
stamens

4
Floral wire

TYPES OF PAPER

CANSON AND MURANO CONSTRUCTION PAPER

Canson construction paper is available in many colors and is just the right weight for making paper-flower leaves (see 8, page 13). It's heavier than craft construction paper and is generally a higher quality. The faintly textured "top" side of the paper adds depth and interest to the leaf, and because it's a matte product, the vein folds of the leaves really stand out. Also, when it is painted, the slight texture gives the paper a more striking appearance. For most projects, I use standard green Canson paper. I also use moss and apple green, or I paint the paper to achieve the exact shade I want (see the Rhododendron, page 50). Murano paper is another brand of art construction paper that comes in the same standard sizes and texture as Canson paper, though the color palette is brighter and more vivid.

DECORATIVE PAPER

Metallic, patterned, splattered, and floral-printed papers are all considered decorative papers. I like to use these papers for highly stylized looks. Feel free to mix and match any decorative papers that appeal to you.

DOUBLETTE CREPE PAPER

Doublette crepe paper is a double-layered alternative to single-layer crepe paper; I use it to make the centers for the Hellebore (page 66), the Easter Lily (page 92), and the Rhododendron (page 50). It is stiff and resilient and has a strong vertical grain that causes the paper to expand when wet. When you bleach the edge, it ruffles, unlike any other paper. It's a good choice for oversize blooms, because it's stiffer than regular tissue and holds up nicely to gravity. The paper is typically two-tone, featuring a different color on each side.

FINE CREPE PAPER

Fine crepe paper is used for more delicate blooms where texture is still needed, like the Cosmos (page 58). I also use it for many of the centers. It, too, has a grain, and, just like tissue paper, it must be cut in the direction of the grain. Fine crepe paper is pliable and has a softening effect on the overall look of the flower. I often buy vintage crepe that has faded into colors that are no longer available.

TISSUE PAPER

Typically available in 20" x 30" (50 x 76 cm) sheets, tissue paper is used for the majority of the flower petals, buds, and centers for the projects in this book. As a material choice, it is the most lifelike—the semi-translucent paper allows light to shine through, just the way the sun shines through petals in nature. Tissue paper is also fragile and will tear just like a real petal, so make sure you handle it carefully.

WORKING WITH PAPER

UNDERSTANDING GRAIN

You may not realize it but paper, like fabric, has a grain. In the manufacturing process, the fibers align in one direction, and this affects what happens when you cut them. When you cut with the grain, the paper folds and generally behaves as you'd like it to. When you cut against the grain, the paper will fight you, curling and twisting. You can identify the grain in paper by looking closely at its fibers to see in which direction they are running. If you are unsure, try folding the ends of the paper so that it bows in the middle—the direction in which your paper is more easily bent is the direction of the grain. You might also find that the paper will tear or fold more easily along the grain.

CUTTING PAPER STRIPS

The way I make sure I'm cutting the petals on the grain is to precut my tissue paper into strips. A precise edge is essential to the final look and feel of the flower, so it's important that your scissors or rotary cutters are sharp, especially when you are cutting petals or leaves. Given that tissue paper is relatively inexpensive, it's best to start over if you end up with a ragged edge.

When I list the materials for making each flower, I provide dimensions for the strips of tissue needed, which I like to cut in batches ahead of time. Tissue paper comes in 20" x 30" (50 x 76 cm) sheets, and the tissue strips in the book are generally either 3" (7.5 cm) or 4" (10 cm) wide, though some are a bit larger, like the 9" (23-cm) wide strips, which I use for the Easter Lily petals on page 94. It's important to cut the strips against the direction of the grain. That way, when you go to cut the petals, you will be cutting with, or in the same direction of, the grain, which is key to making sure the petals behave!

To cut the strips, you'll need a cutting mat, rotary cutter, and quilting ruler. Stack as many tissue sheets as are called for in the directions on your cutting mat, and arrange the

papers so the 20" (50 cm) edge is perpendicular to your cutting board. Cut the stack into the called-for number of sets of 3" x 20" (7.5 x 50 cm) strips. One stack of sheets can also yield three sets of 4" x 20" (10 x 50 cm) strips to make thirty-six 3" (7.5 cm) strips, and eighteen 4" (10 cm) strips. Remember, at this point you are cutting against the grain. When it's time to cut out the petal shape, you will place the template (located in the Templates section on page 162) on the stack of strips, trace the template onto the paper, and cut the shape out in the direction of the grain. If the strips are 30" (76 cm) long, you've cut them the wrong way.

BLEACHING AND DYEING

Bleaching and dyeing paper are wonderful ways to re-create natural effects and play with color. My favorite ways to manipulate tissue paper with bleach and dye are by dip-dyeing fades, "tie-dyeing" stripes, painting freehand designs, and playing with different color combinations. I also love to paint with gouache on petals and leaves (see page 17).

When I dip-dye tissue paper with bleach, I only dip each piece for up to 5 seconds—any longer, and the color will completely fade. Crepe paper can also be bleached, but because there is twice as much paper to bleach, the dipping time is nearly twice as long. In general, the heavier the weight of a paper, the more time it will require in the bleach solution.

I don't like the way black tissue paper looks when bleached, so I simply dip black paper in plain cold water for a more subtle effect. I've gotten more creative with water and now dip all sorts of colors to create a softer texture while still preserving the vibrancy of the hue.

Dipping tissue in dye is very similar to using bleach or water. You dip the tissue for the same amount of time, and hang in batches, just as you would with either bleach or water. However, working with dye takes a little more prep. I usually work in color batches, so I mix all the colors

I'm thinking about using at the same time. If I'm working on a project composed of many blues, I'll dilute the dye with water as I go in order to achieve some petals with a less saturated tone. The beauty of working with dye is that you can create so many different colors on the same strip of tissue.

Whether you're dipping in bleach, water, or dye, it's best to move from dipping to hanging as quickly as possible. I use clothespins on a metal rack set up over a sheet of heavy-gauge plastic and make sure my space is well ventilated. You may also wish to change into clothes you wouldn't mind staining by accident, or cover up with an apron and gloves.

For all the bleaching techniques, gently mix a solution of 1½ cups (360 ml) cold tap water and 1 tablespoon household bleach in a medium-size glass or metal bowl, so the mixture is at least 2" (5 cm) deep. Different brands and types of tissue paper will respond differently to bleach; I recommend starting with this general recipe and then adjusting the solution as needed. Once you have removed the paper from the bleach, it will take a few minutes for the effect to become apparent. If needed, adjust the solution to get the desired effect. If you want a subtler gradient of color, add a bit more water; if you want to create a stronger gradient, add a bit more bleach.

DIP-DYE WITH BLEACH OR FABRIC DYE

This technique will bleach or dye the long edge of a strip of tissue paper, so the petals will have a gradation of color from the base of the petal to the tip. You can bleach or dye one or both sides of the paper. The paper will be less likely to fall apart if you bleach or dye at least 10 sheets at a time.

1 | Gather a stack of at least ten 3" x 20" (7.5 x 50 cm) or 4" x 20" (10 x 50 cm) strips of colored tissue paper. Loosely fold the short end of the tissue paper stack several times until you have a bundle that is easy to hold and easily fits into the bleaching/dyeing dish.

2 | Dip one lengthwise edge of the bundle 1" (2.5 cm) into the liquid for about 3 seconds (**A+B**). Lift it out and let any excess solution drip off, then carefully unfold (but do not separate) the tissue bundle. If you are creating a dyed strip with 3 colors, dip the other lengthwise edge in your second color (**C**).

3 | Hang up the bundle of strips with a clothespin or other type of clip. Be careful when handling the whole bundle; tissue rips easily.

4 | If you'd like to reduce the drying time, use a blow dryer on a low, hot setting. Aim the dryer at your hanging batch of paper and move in a slow, circular motion. Otherwise, allow the paper to air-dry. When the paper is completely dry, store in an airtight container as to protect it from damage and humidity.

DIP-DYE WITH WATER

If you don't want to change the color of the petal, but you do want the delicately crinkled look that is achieved when the tissue paper has gotten wet, you can gather up a bundle of strips, just as you would to bleach or dye the paper, dip them in cold water, and then carefully hang them up to dry.

TIE-DYE WITH BLEACH OR FABRIC DYE

This technique will create a vertical stripe (or stripes, if dyeing) on the petal, which really allows you to experiment with different color combinations.

1 | Gather 1 stack of at least ten 3" x 20" (7.5 x 50 cm) or 4" x 20" (10 x 50 cm) strips of colored tissue paper. Loosely fold it lengthwise in 2" (5 cm) accordion folds. Be careful to not crease the tissue.

2 | Dip 1" (2.5 cm) of the folded edge into the solution for about 3 seconds (**D+E**). Lift it out and let any excess solution drip off, then carefully unfold (but do not separate) the tissue bundle. If you are creating a dyed strip with 3 colors, dip the other folded edge into your second color (**F**).

3 | Hang up the unfolded bundle of tissue strips with a clothespin or other type of clip. Clip the dry edge only, and be careful when handling the whole bundle; tissue rips easily.

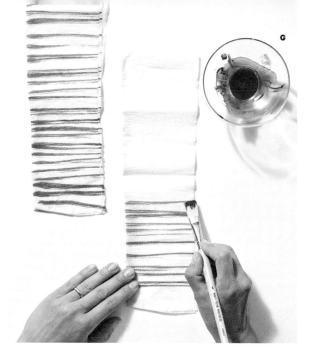

FREEHAND PAINTING WITH BLEACH OR DYE

For many years, I simply painted individual petals or leaves with gouache paint to create the color patterns that appear naturally on real flowers. But when I started taking things up a notch with bolder flowers and more bountiful arrangements, I discovered that it was easier to freehand paint, bleach, dye, and splatter the whole strip of tissue paper first!

When painting whole strips, I layer 2 at a time so that the paint doesn't soak right through the tissue (a single layer would be too weak to hold the color). You can see this effect with the Parrot Tulip on page 104. It's a delicate flower with vibrant stripes on the petals.

1 | Gather 1 stack of two 30" x 20" (76 x 50 cm) sheets of colored tissue paper.

2 | Using a medium-size paintbrush with natural bristles, such as a watercolor brush, paint your design on the paper with the bleach or dye. Try making stripes lengthwise and crosswise, or alternating between thick or thin stripes. Don't worry about applying your bleach or dye perfectly; small drips and uneven lines will make the finished flower more natural-looking (**G**).

3 | Let dry flat for about 20 minutes so the design doesn't run. Then hang up the stack of tissue paper sheets with a clothespin or other type of clip to dry completely. Be careful when handling the sheets; tissue rips easily.

PAINTING PETALS WITH GOUACHE

Many flowers have a bright marking in the center of their petals. This can be accomplished by painting each petal with gouache paint (you can see this effect in the Rhododendron on page 50). Working with two petals at a time, paint a quick swath of color from the middle of the petal to the base and let dry. Similarly, strips can be painted with gouache using horizontal freehand stripes (**G**). To add a speckled paint texture to leaves or petals, mix gouache paint with a few splashes of water to create a thin consistency. Dip a paintbrush with natural bristles into the gouache and do a test run on scrap paper to make sure the paint will splatter. Load the brush with paint and hold the brush 6" to 8" (15 to 20 cm) over the paper. Gently tap the brush handle so the paint splatters evenly on the paper (**H**). Lay the paper flat to dry. (Note that you can create an additional effect using bleach or fabric dye; see pages 15–16.)

PAINTING LEAVES WITH GOUACHE

You can apply paint to leaves either before cutting them out or after. For instance, you can splatter paint onto Canson paper before cutting out the leaves, as is done for the Coleus (see page 122). Or you can cut out the leaves first, and then paint them. However, it's important to paint leaves before folding the veins. Lay the leaves on a piece of newsprint and, using a paintbrush with natural bristles, dab paint in the center of each leaf, and let dry. For a natural effect, use loose, quick strokes.

GETTING STARTED

17

THE EXQUISITE BOOK OF PAPER FLOWER TRANSFORMATIONS

FLOWER CONSTRUCTION BASICS

Once the tissue has been cut into strips and bleached, dyed, or painted, it's time to focus on constructing the flowers—stems, centers, bud balls, petals, and leaves. Though each individual flower has slight variations, the core techniques for constructing all of the blooms are essentially the same.

WORKING WITH WIRE

Wire is the support system for paper flowers, and it's very important to use the proper gauge of wire recommended in the instructions for each project. Substituting wire gauges will compromise the finished look and functionality of the project. You want the flower or plant to be strong but appear delicate, so when it comes to selecting wire, thinner is generally better. On the other hand, there is nothing worse than creating a long, complicated branch that bends and sags once you are finished, because you did not include enough supporting wire in the stems. Unfortunately, if this happens, you can't go back and add more wire; you have to start over.

The thinner the wire, the higher the gauge number, so delicate blooms and leaves will generally be made with 20- to 24-gauge wire. Branches, centers, and reinforcement wires will generally be 16- to 18-gauge. If you have any doubts about the strength of the wire you're using, it can help to test the strength of the stem as you go. Every so often as you are working, hold the stem at the very bottom of the wire and see if the weight of the top is causing the stem to bend. If the top is too heavy, the piece will lean unattractively, even precariously. You should be able to control the whole stem by holding it at the base. If the stem is too weak, add reinforcement wire. You can also use reinforcement wire to round out a stem so that it is uniform in thickness. The directions for each flower include how to add reinforcement wires as needed.

TAPING

Throughout the projects in this book, you'll find that floral tape keeps everything together. It is used to construct blooms and leaves, to attach flowers and leaves to stems, to cover stem wire, and, in some instances, to attach stems to larger branches. With practice, well-executed taping will give your projects a natural appearance. In order to achieve the most natural-looking flowers, the goal is to minimize the amount of tape you use. Buds, centers, sepals, and leaves should all feel secure and sturdy, but use the least amount of tape possible. When taping two stems together, always make sure that they are straight (not twisted), and always bend wires after (not before) they are taped. Once a wire is bent, it is hard to get it truly straight again, and it will appear bumpy and crooked. If you do end up with bent wire, save it to make a Rhododendron branch (see page 50), where thick, bumpy, and crooked look's good!

Floral tape, like many pliable adhesives, contains glue that is only activated once the tape is stretched. I use the standard green tape because it matches the green Canson paper I use for leaves; however, I do use different colored tapes to match or add an accent when the leaf color is a color other than green.

To start, gently stretch about 5" (13 cm) of tape between your fingers and thumbs to release the adhesive. You don't want to stretch too much at a time, because this will cause the tape to lose its stickiness and shape. Keep the tape taut as you apply it to the wire or paper. It's a good idea to practice your taping before attempting to make any flowers—I recommend taping six 18" (46 cm) lengths of 18-gauge wire, applying floral tape from end to end. The goal is to create a smooth, delicate-looking layer of tape.

Don't be discouraged if at first your tape has bumps and wrinkles—taping gets much neater (and easier) with practice.

ANATOMY OF A FLOWER

BUD

PETAL

CENTER

LEAVES

STEM

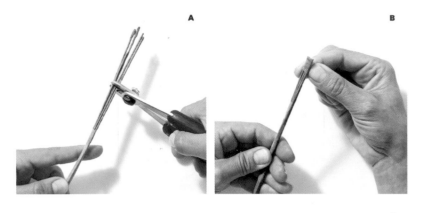

When taping a stem, start at the top, and wrap the tape around and down the wire toward the bottom. To start, hold the stem in your working hand and the tape in the other. Once you have stretched a section of the tape, attach the tape end over the top of the wire; then twist the wire and pinch the tape to it until you have completely covered the end. This requires rolling the tape, then twisting the wire, keeping the tape taut as you twist. Continue by slowly wrapping the tape around the wire diagonally, overlapping the tape edge as little as possible, while tightly pinching the tape to the wire for a clean, neat look. Continue until you have completely covered the wire. When you reach the end, finish by tearing the tape from the roll with enough left to cover almost to the end of the stem. Then pinch and smooth the tape onto the end. Often, for single flowers, the wire ends will be exposed and need to be clipped.

To finish the stem wire, turn the flower upside down and cut the stem to your desired length (**A**). Roll the tape end over the wire end and tightly twist the tape around and onto the exposed wire, pinching it to the wire as you go (**B**). Tape back up the stem for a few inches and break off the tape, pressing it to the stem for a clean, finished look (**C**).

TACKING

There are times when we need to hold a few blooms together without adding any bulk to the main stem. For this we use a method called "tacking." To tack a cluster of blooms, hold the stems together and wrap the floral tape around the stems once or twice for ½" (12 mm).

CENTERS AND BUD BALLS

Many of the flowers in this book begin with a flower center, and we use five main types: pom-pom, poppy, bottlebrush, simple and complex stamen, and bud ball. When you are taping a center, you want it to feel secure and stable. Pinch the center; if you feel movement or sense air between the layers of tape, you should stop and remake the center.

This movement can result if the tape was either not fully activated when you applied it or if it was not applied tightly enough. Remember, maintain tension on the tape when you are working with it, and make sure to press or pinch it into place frequently. This wire will become the main stem of the flower in most cases and should feel very secure.

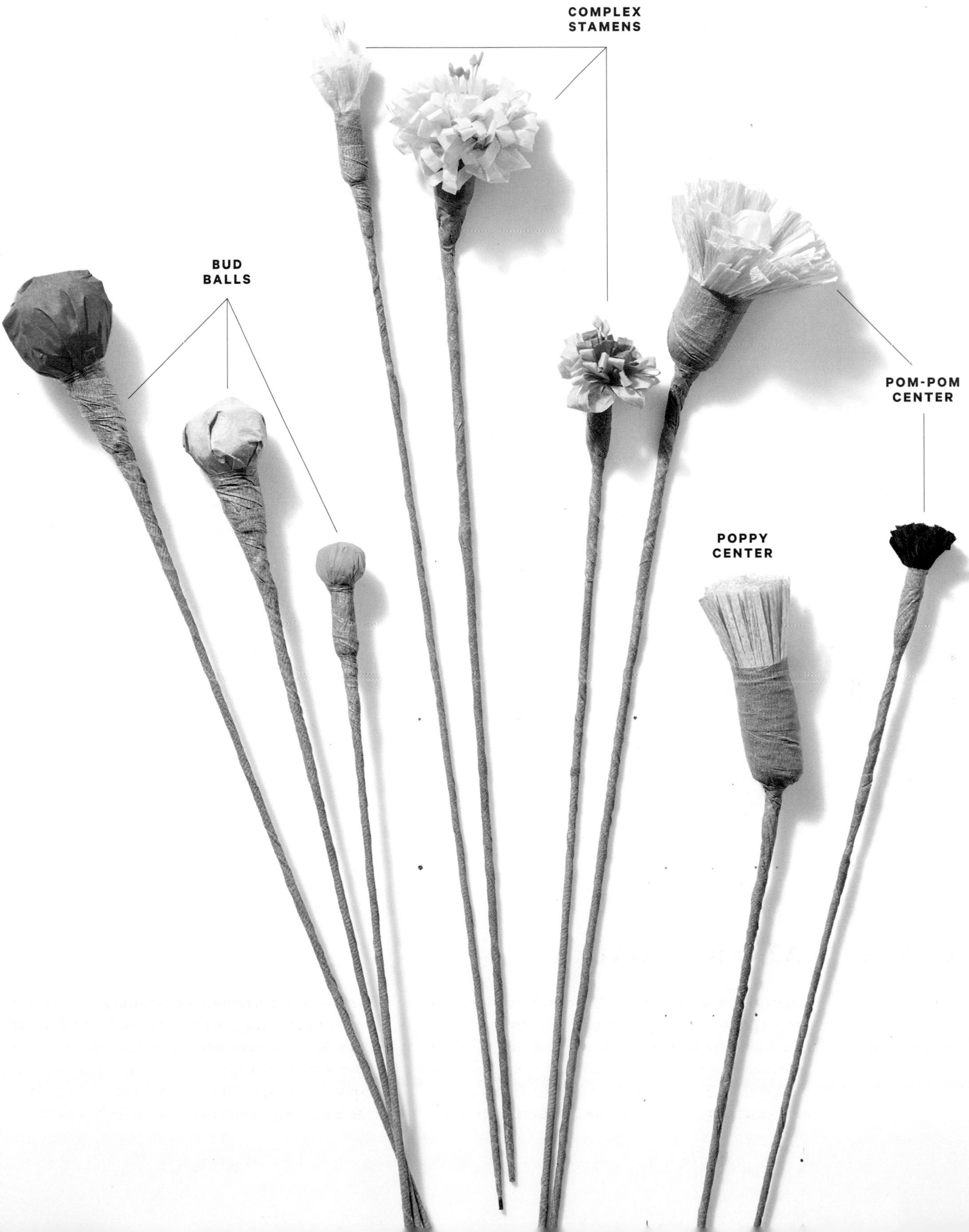

COMPLEX
STAMENS

BUD
BALLS

POM-POM
CENTER

POPPY
CENTER

Pom-Pom Centers

MATERIALS (FOR ALL SIZES)
- Scissors
- Fringing shears (optional)
- Green floral tape
- 9" (23 cm) length 18-gauge pretaped wire
- 1½" x 9" (4 x 23 cm) strip tissue or crepe paper (for small pom-pom); 3" x 20" (7.5 x 50 cm) strip tissue or crepe paper (for medium pom-pom); three 3" x 20" (7.5 x 50 cm) strips tissue or crepe paper (for large pom-pom)

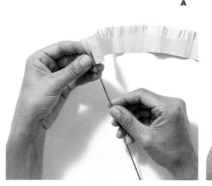

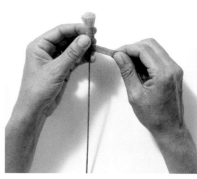

A   **B**   **C**

SMALL POM-POM
Fold the tissue strip in half lengthwise and cut a ½" (12 mm) fringe along the unfolded edge. Working on a smooth, low-friction surface, wrap and press the unfringed edge of the tissue around the wire (**A+B**), and secure it to the wire with green floral tape (**C**). This is now the main flower stem. Fluff and trim the center with scissors as needed.

MEDIUM POM-POM
Fold the tissue strip in half lengthwise, then fold it in half crosswise. Cut a ½" (12 mm) fringe along the unfolded edge. Unfold the crosswise folds so that the strip measures 20" (50 cm) long, but leave the lengthwise fold. Working on a smooth, low-friction surface, wrap and press the unfringed (folded) edge of the tissue around the wire,

and secure it to the wire with green floral tape. This is now the main flower stem. Fluff and trim the center with scissors as needed.

LARGE POM-POM
Fold one tissue strip crosswise into quarters to measure 3" x 5" (7.5 x 13 cm). Cut a 1" (2.5 cm) fringe along the unfolded edge. Unfold the crosswise folds so that the strip measures 3" x 20" (7.5 x 50 cm) again. Working on a smooth, low-friction surface, wrap and press the unfringed edge of the tissue strip in around the wire, and secure it to the wire with green floral tape. Repeat with the remaining 2 strips, wrapping them over the first tissue strip on the wire. This is now the main flower stem. Fluff and trim the center with scissors as needed.

Poppy Center

MATERIALS
- Safety cotton swab
- Scissors
- 9" (23 cm) length 18-gauge pretaped wire
- Two 2" (5 cm) squares tissue paper
- Green floral tape
- 1" x 11" (2.5 x 28 cm) strip Doublette crepe paper
- Fringing shears (optional)

D   **E**   **F**

Trim one end of the cotton swab stick ⅓" (8 mm) from the bulb. Insert the pretaped wire into the hollow of the cotton swab stem and secure it with green floral tape, covering 3" to 4" (7.5 to 10 cm) down the wire. Layer the two squares of tissue paper on top of each other. Place the bulb of the cotton swab in the middle of the tissue square and wrap the tissue completely around the swab (**D**). Secure them tightly

around the base with floral tape. Cut a ⅔" (16 mm) fringe lengthwise down the 1" x 11" (2.5 x 28 cm) strip of crepe paper (cutting with the grain). Gather up the unfringed edge of the crepe paper to create a fan shape. Wrap the gathered fringe evenly around the cotton-swab center, making sure the fringe extends about ¼" (6 mm) above the swab, then secure with floral tape (**E+F**).

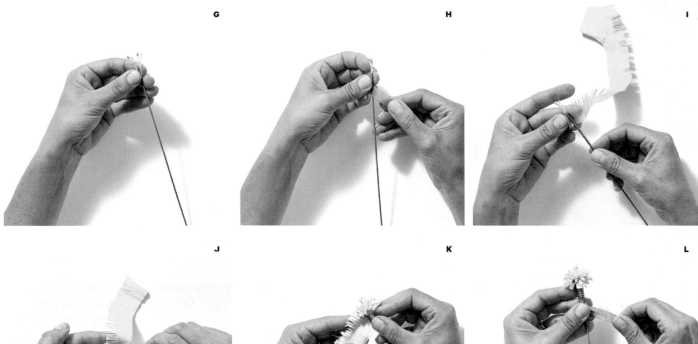

Simple and Complex Stamen

MATERIALS (FOR BOTH STYLES)

- 3 double-headed yellow stamen filaments
- Scissors
- Fringing shears (optional; for complex stamen only)
- 9" (23 cm) length 18-gauge pretaped wire
- Green floral tape
- 1" x 5" (2.5 x 12 cm) strip Doublette crepe paper (for complex stamen only)
- 2" x 11" (5 x 28 cm) strip tissue paper (for complex stamen only)

SIMPLE STAMEN

Fold the stamen filaments in half. Using floral tape, attach the folded end of the stamens to one end of the pretaped wire, wrapping the wire 1½" (4 cm) past the stamens. (**G+H**)

COMPLEX STAMEN

Begin by making a simple stamen. Use scissors or fringing shears to cut a ½" (12 mm) fringe down the length of the crepe paper strip. If you prefer, fold the paper in half crosswise to cut more than one layer at a time. Wrap the crepe paper evenly around the stamens so that the tips extend about ½" (12 mm) above the fringe (**I+J**). Secure the fringed crepe paper by firmly wrapping them with floral tape. Fold the tissue strip in half lengthwise, and cut a ½" (12 mm) fringe along the folded edge. Wrap the tissue evenly around the crepe paper, leaving about ¼" (6 mm) of fringed crepe paper exposed (**K**). Secure the tissue with floral tape just below the fringed edge, and continue wrapping the remaining length of wire (**L**). This is now the main stem.

A

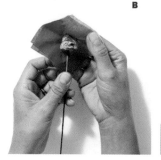
B

C

D

Basic Bud Ball

MATERIALS (FOR ALL SIZES)
- Green floral tape
- 9" (23 cm) length pretaped 18-gauge wire
- Scissors
- Tissue paper cut to the appropriate sizes

The basic bud ball is not technically a center—it is a flower bud that is about to open. But the method for making bud balls is very similar to making centers. We've included the instructions for how to make small, medium, and large bud balls here, but you can vary the size of the paper to create buds of assorted sizes.

SMALL BUD
1" x 1" (2.5 x 2.5 cm) square for the center; 1½" x 1½" (4 x 4 cm) square for the outer layer

MEDIUM BUD
3" x 4" (7.5 x 10 cm) piece for the center; two 2" x 2" (5 x 5 cm) squares for the outer layer

LARGE BUD
3" x 20" (7.5 x 50 cm) strip for the center; two 3" x 3" (7.5 x 7.5 cm) squares for the outer layer

For all sizes, crumple the piece of tissue for the bud center into a ball (**A**). Hold it in place at one end of the wire. For the small bud, wrap the ball completely with one piece of outer layer tissue paper, creating a smooth, wrinkle-free surface. For medium and large buds, use two pieces of tissue paper for the outer layer, maintaining a smooth surface (**B**). Firmly grasping the paper edges, use floral tape to attach the bud to the taped wire (**C**). Hold the ball in one hand while wrapping the floral tape around the base with the other, taping, pinching, and turning the stem as you go (**D**). Again, make sure to maintain a smooth, wrinkle-free surface.

PETALS

Petal shapes vary from flower to flower, but the manner for making them into blooms is relatively similar (the petal templates are located on pages 162 to 172). Generally speaking, a fluid cut using sharp scissors is essential to making a lovely petal, and petals must be cut in the direction of the paper's grain. Because I usually make more than one project at a time, I often prepare my tissue strips in bulk ahead of time (see page 14). This way, there is never a question about which direction the grain is going in when I'm ready to cut out the petals.

To trace and cut out the petals, take the number of precut strips specified in the flower instructions and place the petal template on the strips so that the top of the petal is oriented along the lengthwise edge of the strip. Trace the petal template onto the strip as many times as is necessary for the quantity of petals you need, then cut out the shapes.

SCULPTING PETALS
Before attaching a petal to a stem, you will sometimes need to "sculpt" it to give it a shape. The overall goal is to give the paper dimension and texture—sharp creases or folds are rarely called for. Here are some techniques I use to create natural shapes with my petals.

E

F

G

H

I

J

SHAPING WITH A SCISSOR EDGE

Scissors are a quick and handy tool I use to add curl to petals. You can do this with a single petal or stacked petals (but always curl before you dart) (**E**). Gently pull the paper between your thumb and the closed edge of the scissor blade, increasing or lessening the tension as you pull for a tight or a gentle curl (**F**). Note that this technique also works well for curling leaves and sepals.

CREATING A DART

A dart is a triangular fold that is used to create a natural cupped shape in tissue petals, much the way a fabric dart creates contour in a sewn garment. The paper dart is especially helpful for creating volume in double-layered petals. This fold extends the length of the petal, from the bottom to just below the top. The base of the dart should fold ½" (12 mm), creating a tapered triangular shape (**G+H**). Gently pinch the base of the petal to give it a cupped appearance (**I+J**).

TAPING PETALS

When taping petals to the stem, it is especially important to use as little tape as possible without compromising the strength of the flower. Be sure to tape each petal at the same place vertically on the stem so that the length of the flower base remains the same after each petal is attached.

Your first revolution of tape is called your tapeline. Make sure that you tape each additional petal in place on top of the tapeline that already exists, rather than moving down the stem (when I teach paper flower making, this is one of the most common mistakes beginners make). You do not want to be inching down the stem and have the petals attached progressively lower or you will end up with a strange, elongated bloom.

When adding small groupings of petals, tape just twice around the base, angling your tape toward the bottom of the flower with each turn. Again, make sure that you tape each additional petal in place on top of the tapeline that already exists. If you tape the petal to the same tape layer, the bloom will not be secure; it will slip and rotate as you continue to tape additional petals. This is not a problem that can be fixed later, so if this is the situation, it's best to start over. With practice, taping petals will feel like second nature. If you are creating a flower that has multiple blooms, you may find it helpful to stand the completed blooms in a small bottle so they don't get crushed while you work.

LEAVES AND SEPALS

Like with the petals I make, I try to translate the beauty of natural leaves to paper. For example, I gently bend—and never crease—the paper to create the look of veins, and I very rarely bend a vein fold in a straight line, instead opting to meander slightly from center to edge for a more organic shape. I use leaves to fill in spaces on the stem where flowers will not fit, and they serve to balance out and soften the vivid blooms. Sepals are a type of leaf that cover the bud, protecting it as it grows. As the bud begins to unfurl, the sepals remain attached at the base of the bud. You can see a sepal in the Hellebore on page 66.

In this book, each flower project with a leaf or leaves will include specific details regarding the style, size, and quantity.

Before cutting out leaves, it helps to trim the paper down to manageable pieces, and then cut each leaf individually. I like to use Canson paper to make all of my leaves. Canson paper is like fabric in that it has a right side (a subtle, pulpy texture on the top) and a wrong side (a smooth, uniform finish on the bottom). When you are folding and cutting, it's important to be aware which side is which. Once you have made a few projects and feel comfortable with the process, experiment with cutting shapes freehand, as I do. I also recommend using a photocopier to increase and decrease the size of the templates to create a wide variety of leaf sizes, just as you would find in nature.

MATERIALS

- Leaf template of your choice (see pages 162 to 172)
- 19" x 25" (48 x 63.5 cm) sheet green Canson paper
- Scissors
- Hot glue gun
- Hot glue sticks
- 9" (23 cm) length 18-gauge pretaped wire (Note: Some leaves use 20-gauge wire. Check the flower's individual instructions before beginning.)
- ½" x 2" (12 mm x 5 cm) piece light-green tissue paper
- Green floral tape

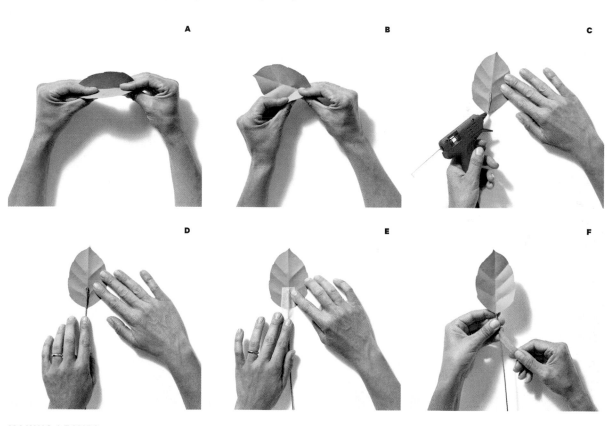

MAKING LEAVES

These instructions apply to all types of leaves used in this book. The process will quickly become second nature after you've done it a few times, but remember not to overtape or bend the wires before you tape them!

1 | Trace or photocopy the leaf template and cut out the shape. Trace around the template onto the Canson paper, then cut out the traced leaf shape. Gently crease (but do not fold) the leaf along the guidelines provided on the template to create veins (**A+B**).

2 | Using the glue gun, apply a line of hot glue to the underside of the leaf (the smooth side of the paper) from the middle center to the base. Attach the wire to the back of the leaf by placing it in the glue (**C+D**).

3 | While the glue is still sticky, place the light-green tissue strip over the wire and leaf area, making sure that half is covering the wire on the leaf and half is covering the stem (**E**). Gently pinch the tissue paper to the stem once the glue has dried, after about 3 to 5 minutes. Apply floral tape starting just beneath the base of the leaf, covering the remaining length of exposed wire (**F**).

PART 1

THE FLOWERS

01

ALLIUM

I love the whimsical magic of the allium bloom, which grows
from the stalks of garlic plants. When I was younger,
my family grew garlic, which we braided and sold at farmers'
markets in California. Once the plants went to seed, I would
cut the geometric blooms that were left behind and fill
vases around the house with them. In paper form, you can enjoy
these oversize structural blooms without the odor.

GENERAL MATERIALS

- Scissors
- Green floral tape
- Assorted fabric dyes
- Wire cutters
- Fifteen 18" lengths 18-gauge reinforcement wires

FOR PETALS

- Nine 3" x 20" (7.5 x 50 cm) strips chartreuse tissue paper dip-dyed with bleach

FOR SIMPLE STAMEN CENTERS

- 50 double-headed orange filament stamens
- Fifty 9" (23 cm) lengths 20-gauge wire, pretaped with green floral tape

ALLIUM

FINISHED SIZE
Approximately 21" (53 cm)

1

PREPARE MATERIALS

Photocopy or trace the Allium petal template on page 169 and cut out the petal shape. Cut fifty 3" x 3" (7.5 x 7.5 cm) pieces from the chartreuse tissue paper strips and place them in 10 stacks of 5 pieces each. Trace the template onto each stack of tissue and cut them out to make 50 petals.

Create 50 simple stamen centers with the orange filament stamens, following the instructions on page 23.

2

SHAPE CONNECTED PETAL

Working on a smooth, low-friction surface, gently gather the bottom edge of the connected petal into a fanlike shape with your fingertips (**A**). Position the connected petal flush to the tip of one of the simple stamen center wires so that the stamens extend above the paper by ½" (12 mm) (**B**). Make sure that you don't see any of the actual wire, just the stamen. Adjust the petal ends so that they are evenly spaced and overlap slightly at their base. Attach the connected petal with floral tape (**C**). Set this aside and repeat with remaining 49 petals and simple stamen centers. Bend each stem at a 60-degree angle 2½" (6 cm) below each floret (**D**).

3

ASSEMBLE BLOOM

Place 3 florets with their stems flush, positioning the angled point of the second and third floret stems 1" (2.5 cm) down from the angled point of the first floret's stem and attach them with floral tape (**E**). Repeat with the remaining floret, placing them around the first two to create a ball shape (**F+G**). As you attach the florets, add in approximately 15 reinforcement wires to thicken and elongate the stem. To attach, place the reinforcement wire alongside the main stem and insert the top of the wire into the base of the bloom (**H**). When you are finished adding flowers, rearrange and bend the stems to create a global shape. Wrap it with floral tape the full length of the stem. Turn the flower upside down, cut the stem to your desired length, and wrap the cut stem end with floral tape to finish.

02
CHARM PEONY

Everybody adores peonies, and they're one of the flowers I've
been making since the beginning. My earlier peonies were much
more stylized, but lately, I've wanted something different and
more realistic. This version feels more natural to me, especially the
petals. Before, I used scalloping shears to shape their edges.
Now, I hand-cut the petals so I can vary the size and shape.
When you make this flower, try to make an assortment of petals
and mix them all together in one bloom. Make some blooms using
a double-petal, some a triple-petal, or even just a single petal.
You'll see how wonderfully fluffy they are in the end.

GENERAL MATERIALS

- Scissors
- Green floral tape
- 18" (46 cm) length 18-gauge reinforcement wire
- Wire cutters

FOR PETALS

- Six 4" x 20" (10 x 50 cm) strips coral tissue paper, dip-dyed with bleach (see page 00)

FOR CENTERS

- Three 3" x 20" (7.5 x 50 cm) strips soft pink tissue paper, dip-dyed with water (see page 16)
- One 3" x 20" (7.5 x 50 cm) strip burgundy tissue paper, dip-dyed with water (see page 16)
- 18" (46 cm) length 18-gauge pretaped wire

FOR LEAVES

- 19" x 25" (48 x 63.5 cm) sheet green Canson paper
- Hot glue gun
- Hot glue sticks
- Two 9" (23 cm) lengths pretaped 20-gauge wire
- Two ½" x 2" (12 mm x 5 cm) pieces light-green tissue paper

CHARM PEONY

FINISHED SIZE
Approximately 20" (50 cm)

PREPARE MATERIALS

Photocopy or trace the Charm Peony Large Petal template and Small Petal template on page 165 and cut out the petal shapes. For the large petals, cut twenty 4" x 5" (10 x 13 cm) pieces from 5 of the petal tissue paper strips. Divide them into 2 stacks of 10. Place the Large Petal template on 1 stack so the top of the petal is at the bleach-dipped edge of the paper. Trace the template onto the tissue. Repeat with the second stack. For the small petals, cut five 4" x 1½" (10 x 4 cm) pieces from the remaining petal tissue strip. Trace the Small Petal template onto the tissue. Cut them all out to make a total of 20 large and 5 small petals.

Photocopy or trace the Charm Peony Center Petal and Fleck Petal templates on page 165 and cut out the shapes. Cut fifteen 3" x 2¾" (7.5 x 7 cm) pieces from the soft pink tissue paper strips. Divide them into 3 stacks of 5. Place the Center Petal template on 1 stack so the top of the petal is at the water-dipped edge of the paper. Trace the template onto the top tissue, cut out the stack, and then repeat with the remaining 2 stacks to make a total of 15 center petals. Repeat the process with the burgundy tissue paper and Fleck Petal template to create 3 fleck petals.

Photocopy or trace the Peony Leaf templates on page 165 and cut out the leaf shapes. Trace 1 small and 2 large leaves onto green Canson paper and cut them out. Construct the leaf stems following the instructions on page 27.

CREATE CENTER

Working on a smooth, low-friction surface, gently gather the bottom edge of a center petal into a fanlike shape with your fingertips (**A**). Attach the gathered edge of the petals ¼" (6 mm) down the stem to a pretaped wire with floral tape (**B**). The top edge of the first piece of tape that you wrap is your tapeline. Repeat with the remaining center petals, overlapping each with the one before by ½" (12 mm) in a radiating fashion evenly around the wire to create a round floret. Add in the flecks randomly as you go (**C**).

SHAPE AND CREATE SINGLE, DOUBLE-, OR TRIPLE-PETALS

To give the small petals a cupped shape, add a dart to each (see page 25). The 3-point fold for the dart should extend from the bottom of the petal to ½" (12 mm) from the top (**D**). The base of the dart fold should measure about ¼" (6 mm) across and taper to a point. Gently pinch the base of each petal to give it a cupped appearance (**E**).

To create double- or triple-petals with the large petals, place one large petal on top of another—or on top of 2 others for a triple-petal—then fan them apart ½" (12 mm). To give the double- or triple-petal a cupped shape, add a dart as above. Repeat to make a total of 10 large double- or triple-petals. (Note: You will have to cut additional petals in step 1 for the triple-petal effects.)

CONSTRUCT BLOOM

The small petals are meant to act as a progression between the inner (center) and outer (large) petals. Attach the first small petal to the center stem with floral tape, wrapping the tape down and around the wire twice (**F**). Attach the remaining 4 small petals randomly around the center in the same way.

Place the gathered end of one large double-petal at the base of the center. Attach it with floral tape, wrapping the tape to about 1" (2.5 cm) beyond the base of the center. Place a second double-petal alongside the first, overlapping the edges by ½" (12 mm) in a radiating fashion. The peony will look more natural if you add the petals more randomly. Double back and add one under the first two. Add one opposite the first grouping and then fill in where needed (**G**). Maintaining the tapeline, wrap the base with floral tape. Repeat with the remaining double-petals, wrapping the base of each with floral tape beginning at the tapeline and encircling the center. The overhead view of the flower should be balanced. As you place the last double-petal, make sure the overall shape of the bloom is round. Fluff and open the bloom, adjusting petals as needed to give the flower a natural look.

ASSEMBLE STEM

Place the reinforcement wire alongside the main stem and insert the top end of the wire into the base of the bloom (**H**). Holding it flush to the main stem, attach the reinforcement wire to the stem by wrapping it with floral tape the full length of the flower stem. Bend the constructed bloom at a 60-degree angle at its base.

Bend each leaf at a 60-degree angle at its base. Place the small leaf stem flush to the main stem, positioning the leaf 2" (5 cm) below the bloom (**I**). Attach the leaf to the main stem with floral tape, wrapping it to 2" (5 cm) below the base of the leaf. Repeat with the 2 large leaf stems, positioning the leaf on opposite sides and 2" (5 cm) below the small leaf. Wrap to the bottom of the stem. Using wire cutters, trim the flower stem to 4" (10 cm) below the bottom leaf. Turn the flower upside down and wrap the cut stem end with floral tape to finish.

03
EDEN ROSE

Although I love the fanciful garden rose from my first book, roses are popular flowers, and clients often want more realistic interpretations of them. I thought a lot about how to translate what I was literally seeing onto paper, and came up with the natural-looking Eden Rose. Instead of a stylized stamen, the Eden Rose doesn't have a traditional center—you can't see it on the bloom. This flower can be created in a variety of sizes, too, which makes it a perfect choice for a more complex project with multiple blooms, like a branch. Try playing around with different configurations as you make yours.

GENERAL MATERIALS

- Scissors
- Green floral tape
- 18" (46 cm) length 18-gauge reinforcement wire
- Wire cutters

FOR PETALS

- Six 3" x 20" (7.5 x 50 cm) strips yellow tissue paper, dip-dyed fuchsia (see page 16)

FOR EDEN ROSE CENTER (LARGE BUD BALL)

- 20" x 30" (50 x 76 cm) sheet yellow tissue paper (or use leftovers from the petals)
- One 18" (46 cm) length 18-gauge pretaped wire

FOR LEAVES

- 19" x 25" (48 x 63.5 cm) sheet green Canson paper
- Hot glue gun
- Hot glue sticks
- Four 9" (23 cm) lengths 18-gauge pretaped wire
- Four ½" x 2" (12 mm x 5 cm) pieces light-green tissue paper

EDEN ROSE

FINISHED SIZE
Approximately 13" (33 cm)

1

PREPARE MATERIALS

Photocopy or trace the Eden Rose Small, Medium, and Large Petal templates on page 169 and cut out the petal shapes. Cut thirty-four 3" x 3" (7.5 x 7.5 cm) pieces from the tissue paper strips. Stack the pieces into 2 piles of 12 and 1 of 10, and place the small petal template on one stack of 12 so the top of the petal is at the dip-dyed edge of the paper. Trace the template onto the tissue and cut it out to make 12 small petals. Repeat with the medium and large petal templates for the remaining stacks, tracing and cutting 10 medium and 12 large petals, for a total of 34 petals.

Construct a large bud ball to use as the center following the instructions on page 24. Place a reinforcement wire alongside the bud stem and insert the top of the wire into the base of the bud (**A**). Attach it by wrapping it with floral tape the full length of the flower stem.

For the leaves, photocopy or trace the Eden Rose Leaf templates on page 169 and cut out the leaf shapes. Trace 2 small and 2 large leaves onto the green Canson paper and cut them out. Assemble the leaf stems following the instructions on page 27.

2

CREATE DOUBLE-PETALS

Place 1 small petal on top of another, then fan them apart ½" (12 mm) to make a double-petal (**B**). Using the edge of a closed pair of scissors, shape the top edge of three of the double-petals, creating a gentle curl inward (see page 25) (**C**). To give the small double-petals a cupped shape, add a dart (see page 25) (**D**). The 3-point fold for the dart should extend from the bottom of the petals to ½" (12 mm) from the top. The base of the dart fold should measure about ¼" (6 mm) across and taper to a point. Gently gather the base of each small double-petal to give it a cupped shape. Repeat with the remaining small petals to make a total of 6 small double-petals.

Place 1 medium petal on top of another, then fan them apart ½" (12 mm) to make a double-petal. Using the edge of a closed pair of scissors, shape the top edge of the double-petal, creating a gentle curl outward (see page 25). To give the medium double-petals a cupped shape, add a dart as above. Repeat with the remaining medium petals to make a total of 5 medium double-petals.

Create 6 large double-petals in the same manner used for the medium double-petals, curling and darting as you did above.

3

CONSTRUCT BLOOM

Place the first small double-petal at the base of the large bud ball center, positioning it so that the petal obscures the top of the bud ball center. Position a second small double-petal opposite the first petal at the same angle so that the first petal swirls inside of it to create a pleasing, spiraled center (**E**). Secure both petals in place with floral tape, wrapping the tape down and around the wire twice, to about ½" (12 mm) below the base. Where you begin to wrap the tape is the tapeline. Repeat with the remaining small double-petals to encircle the center tightly; make sure to begin taping each at the tapeline that you established with the first set.

Place the gathered end of one medium double-petal opposite the base of the last small double-petal. The top of the petal should be ¼" (6 mm) above the small double-petal center you just created. Because these petals are darted and curled, they create the center volume of the rose. Add the remaining medium double-petals, gradually encircling the center and turning the bloom with the addition of each petal, spacing them to create a full, round shape (**F**).

Attach the large double-petals in the same manner as the medium. There should be no sparsely petaled areas (**G**). Fluff the layers of petals to open the bloom. Bend the flower stem forward at a 30-degree angle at the base of the bloom.

4

ASSEMBLE THE STEM

Bend the first large leaf stem at a 60-degree angle and attach it 3" (7.5 cm) below the flower base. Bend two small leaf stems at 60-degree angles, and attach them to each side of the remaining large leaf to create a leaf cluster. Attach the leaf cluster to the opposite side of the main stem 1½" (4 cm) below the first leaf (**H+I**). Using wire cutters, trim the flower to the desired length. Turn the flower upside down and wrap the cut stem end with floral tape to finish.

04
FLUFFY POPPY

If you remember the filler fluff from my first book, this little
cutie will be familiar to you. Although it's fun to
create big, show-stopping blooms, I also love making sweet and
simple options for filling in the spaces of an arrangement,
so that the other, more interesting blooms can take center stage.

**GENERAL
MATERIALS**

- Scissors
- Green floral tape
- 9" (23 cm) length
18-gauge pretaped wire
- Wire cutters

FOR PETALS

- Two 3" x 20"
(7.5 x 50 cm) strips
teal tissue paper,
dip-dyed with bleach
(see page 16)

FLUFFY POPPY

FINISHED SIZE
Approximately 12" (30.5 cm)

PREPARE MATERIALS

To create soft, crinkled petals, place 1 tissue strip on top of the other to make a double layer. Holding the tissue crosswise in the palm of your hand, slowly gather it up, crumpling the strip as you gather (**A**). Be sure to keep the crumples straight—you are not making a ball. Squeeze the piece in your hand (**B**). Unfurl and separate the tissue strips. Working on a smooth, low-friction surface, gently gather 1 tissue strip with your fingertips (**C**), then squeeze the piece in your hand again. It should open up to resemble a loose accordion fold. Repeat with the second tissue strip.

CONSTRUCT BLOOM

Pinch the end of one petal into a fan shape—this will become your first petal. Hold the pinched end to the pretaped wire so that it covers the entire space around (**D**). Wrap with floral tape down and around the wire to about 1" (2.5 cm) beyond the base (**E**). Nestle the second petal beneath the first and attach with floral tape evenly around the wire to create a round floret. Tape the stem the full length of the wire (**F**). Using wire cutters, trim the stem to the desired length. Turn the flower upside down and wrap the cut stem end with floral tape to finish.

A

B

C

D

E

F

05
HYDRANGEA

When I started painting paper and experimenting with dyes, I knew I had to try to make hydrangeas. The antique hydrangeas that appear in the fall are really interesting in color and texture, and I knew speckled dyed paper would add a visual dimension that would translate well for these delicate petals. A hydrangea blossom is made up of many tiny blooms, and it was a challenge to develop a project that wasn't super labor intensive. The leaves here are functional as well as beautiful—they frame the dome-shaped cluster of florets to protect the flowers from getting smashed if the stem is laid on the table.

GENERAL MATERIALS

- Scissors
- Green floral tape
- Wire cutters

FOR PETALS

- Four 3" x 20" (7.5 x 50 cm) strips blue tissue paper, dip-dyed with bleach (see page 16)
- Thirty 9" (23 cm) lengths 20-gauge pretaped wire

FOR SIMPLE STAMEN CENTERS

- 24 double-headed yellow stamen filaments
- Twenty-four 9" (23 cm) lengths 20-gauge pretaped wire

FOR LEAVES

- 19" x 25" (48 x 63.5 cm) sheet green Canson paper
- Hot glue gun
- Hot glue sticks
- Four 9" (23 cm) lengths 18-gauge pretaped wire
- Four ½" x 2" (12 mm x 5 cm) pieces light-green tissue paper

HYDRANGEA

FINISHED SIZE
Approximately 12" (30.5 cm)

1

PREPARE MATERIALS

Photocopy or trace the Hydrangea Petal template on page 162 and cut out the connected petal shape. Cut twenty-four 3" x 3" (7.5 x 7.5 cm) pieces from the blue tissue paper strips. Trace the template onto the tissue (I oriented some with the top at the blue edge and some with the top at the white edge) and cut it out to make 24 connected petals. Because these are simple connected petals, try stacking a few pieces of tissue on top of each other and cut out the stack to save yourself some time.

Create 24 simple stamen centers following the instructions on page 23.

Photocopy or trace the Hydrangea Leaf template on page 162 and cut out the leaf shape. Trace 4 leaves onto the green Canson paper and cut them out. Assemble the leaf stems following the instructions on page 27.

2

SHAPE CONNECTED PETAL

Working on a smooth, low-friction surface, gently gather the bottom edge of a connected petal into a fanlike shape with your fingertips (**A**). Position the connected petal about ½" (12 mm) below the top of the stamen of one of the simple stamen centers (you don't want to see any of the actual wire, just the stamen!) (**B**). Adjust the petal ends so that they are evenly spaced. Because they are gathered, they will overlap slightly at the base. Attach the connected petal with floral tape (**C**). Repeat with the remaining 23 petals and 23 simple stamen centers to create a total of 24 blooms. Bend each stem at a 15-degree angle ¾" (2 cm) below the bloom.

3

ASSEMBLE FLORETS

The general form of the finished flower is dome-shaped, with thicker, branch-like stems. Begin by tacking (see page 20) 3 florets together with floral tape at the point where each is bent. Wrap the tape once around the stems about 2" (5 cm) down the stem. Repeat with the remaining florets to create 8 clusters of 3.

Select one cluster and attach another cluster to it with floral tape. Bend the second cluster outward at a 15-degree angle ¾" (2 cm) below the base of the first grouping (**D**). Repeat with a third cluster, adjusting and positioning the individual flowers as you go to create the desired dome shape (**E**). Using wire cutters, trim 5 of the 9 wires 1" (2.5 cm) down the stem (**F**). Repeat with the remaining 5 clusters, attaching them to the main stem, filling in the space on the stem that you created in trimming the wires so that the stem is smooth. Reposition flowers as you go (**G**).

4

ASSEMBLE STEM

Select 2 leaves and tape them together to create a small branch (**H**). Attach it 1" (2.5 cm) below the floret clusters to frame the back of the flower (**I**). Bend the main stem forward a bit. Tape 2 more leaves together to create a small branch, and attach the branch to the left side of the bloom 1" (2.5 cm) below and opposite the first set of leaves. Using wire cutters, trim the flower stem to 5" (13 cm) below the lowest leaf. Turn the flower upside down and wrap the cut stem end with floral tape to finish.

A

B

C

D

E

F

G

H

I

06
RHODODENDRON

I've learned that if your rhododendrons can survive two winters, they will live forever. In fact, it may be tough to kill them. Thankfully in paper, you don't have to wait out this extended time trial. When I design a large-scale arrangement, I like to use rhododendron branches to create an interesting texture. Their form is unusual and beautifully structural—a large, round, delicate cluster of speckled flowers is framed by dark, spiky green leaves. It's an easy stem to create, and it is easily customizable by painting the leaves and the tissue.

GENERAL MATERIALS
- Scissors
- Fringing shears (optional)
- Green floral tape
- Wire cutters

FOR PETALS
- Eight 4" x 20" (10 x 50 cm) strips hot pink tissue paper, dip-dyed with bleach (see page 16)

FOR COMPLEX STAMEN CENTERS
- 24 double-headed yellow stamen filaments
- Twelve 12" x 9" (30.5 x 23 cm) lengths 18-gauge pretaped wire
- Twelve 1" x 5" (2.5 x 13 cm) strips yellow Doublette crepe paper

FOR LEAVES
- 19" x 25" (48 x 63.5 cm) sheet green Canson paper
- Hot glue gun
- Hot glue sticks
- Nine 4" (10 cm) lengths 20-gauge pretaped wire
- Nine ½" x 2" (12 mm x 5 cm) pieces light-green tissue paper
- Paintbrush
- Blue-green gouache paint

RHODODENDRON

FINISHED SIZE
Approximately 12" (30.5 cm)

PREPARE MATERIALS

Photocopy or trace the Rhododendron Petal template on page 167 and cut out the petal shape. Cut the petal tissue strips into twenty-four 3" x 5" (7.5 x 13 cm) pieces. Position the petal template to get the desired dye effect on the petal. Trace the template onto the tissue and cut out the petal shapes to make 12 connected petals.

Construct 12 complex stamen centers following the instructions on page 23, without including the steps for outer tissue paper.

Photocopy or trace the Rhododendron Leaf template on page 168 and cut out the leaf shape. Paint the Canson paper blue-green, let dry, and trace 9 leaves onto the paper and cut them out.

SHAPE CONNECTED DOUBLE PETALS

Working on a smooth, low-friction surface, gently gather the bottom edge of a connected double-petal into a fanlike shape with your fingertips (**A**). Position the connected double-petal about 1" (2.5 cm) down one of the center stems so the stamens are even with the petal ends and are visible when the flower is viewed from the side (**B**). Adjust the petal ends so that they are evenly spaced and overlap slightly at their base. Attach the connected double-petal with floral tape (**C**). Shape the bloom by pulling at the paper so that it looks and feels balanced. Repeat 11 more times to create a total of 12 florets.

ASSEMBLE BLOOM CLUSTER

Bend 2 florets at a 60-degree angle 2" (5 cm) from the base of the buds and attach them to a third floret at the point where the stems are bent to create a 3-floret cluster (**D**). Wrap the floral tape down and around the stems about 2" (5 cm) below the base. Select 4 more florets and bend them each at a 60-degree angle 2" (5 cm) below the base of the bud, then attach them to the 3-floret cluster stem at the same point where the stems are bent (**E+F**). Adjust them in a pleasing manner around the blooms. Repeat with the remaining 5 florets to make one large bloom cluster.

ASSEMBLE STEM

Bend each of the 12 leaves at a 60-degree angle. Position a leaf so that it frames the flower 2" (5 cm) below the flower cluster and attach with floral tape (**G**). Repeat with the remaining 11 leaves descending the length of the stem (**H+I**). Using wire cutters, trim the stem to 6" (15 cm) below the final leaf set. Turn the flower upside down and wrap the cut stem end with floral tape to finish.

07
CORNFLOWER

When I worked at *Martha Stewart Living*, I created a bridal bouquet that was inspired by the movie *A Room with a View*. It's such a romantic film, and cornflowers always remind me of the scene where the ladies made wreaths for themselves from the field of red poppies and cornflowers. The bouquet I made was ahead of its time, but thankfully, my boss loved it, and it turned out to be one of my most popular pieces. Cornflowers are so simple and beautiful—I know you'll love them, too.

GENERAL MATERIALS

- Scissors
- Fringing shears (optional)
- Green floral tape
- Wire cutters

FOR BLOOMS

- Four 3" x 20" (7.5 x 50 cm) strips french blue tissue paper, handpainted blue (see page 17)
- Zigzag scissors (optional)

FOR SMALL POM-POM CENTERS

- 20" x 60" (50 x 152 cm) sheet black fine crepe paper
- Two 18" (46 cm) lengths 20-gauge pretaped wire

FOR BUD

- 18" (46 cm) length 20-gauge pretaped wire

FOR LEAVES

- 19" x 25" (48 x 63.5 cm) sheet green Canson paper

CORNFLOWER

FINISHED SIZE
Approximately 20" (50 cm)

1

PREPARE MATERIALS

Cut along the center of each 3" x 20" (7.5 x 50 cm) tissue paper strip in a zigzag pattern to create eight 1½" x 20" (4 x 50 cm) strips with one zigzag edge. Each strip will become one petal. Alternatively, you can use the Cornflower Petal template on page 164 as a guide. Set aside one to be used for the bud (you will have one extra).

Photocopy or trace the Cornflower Leaf templates on page 164 and cut out the leaf shapes. Trace an assortment of 10 to 15 leaves onto the green Canson paper and cut them out.

Construct 2 small pom-pom centers using black fine crepe paper following the instructions on page 22.

2

CONSTRUCT BLOOM

Working on a smooth, low-friction surface, gently gather one tissue strip into a fanlike shape with your fingertips (**A**). Pinch the straight edge of the petal into a fan shape and hold the pinched end just below the pom-pom center (**B+C**). Attach the petal to the stem so that it covers no more than half of the space around the stem. Wrap the floral tape down and around the wire to about 1" (2.5 cm) beyond the base. The top layer of floral tape is your tapeline. Place the second petal where the first petal ends, overlapping their edges by ½" (12 mm) and encircling the other half of the stem. Wrap the base with floral tape, making sure to start your tape at the same point on the stem, the tapeline. Repeat with a third petal, staggering it below the first 2 petals (**D**). Fluff the petals by gently pushing them down so that the center is visible. Repeat to make a second bloom with 3 petals.

3

CONSTRUCT BUD

Pinch one end of the bud petal into a fan shape as you did with the bloom petals and hold the pinched end. Attach the petal to the stem so that it wraps completely around the stem (**E**). Wrap with floral tape down and around the wire to about 1" (2.5 cm) beyond the base.

4

ASSEMBLE STEM

The complete stem is composed of 2 bloom stems and one bud stem. When assembling the complete stem, you'll add leaves to each blossom and bud first, then connect the 3 stems, and finally tie the whole piece together with more leaves. To begin, shape the leaves by pulling each one lengthwise between your thumb and middle finger, creating a natural curl (**F**). Place a leaf flush to one of the bloom stems, positioning the bottom end of the leaf 1" (2.5 cm) below the base of the bloom. Using floral tape, attach the leaf to the bloom stem by pressing the bottom portion of the leaf paper to the stem so it forms to the shape of the stem and tape the bottom ¼" (6 mm) of the leaf to the stem. Repeat with a second leaf, positioning it opposite and ½" (12 mm) below the first leaf. Continue attaching leaves in this manner, alternating down the stem every ½" (12 mm) or so. Repeat with the second bloom and bud stems.

Position a bud stem so that the bud appears slightly taller than the first bloom. Attach the bud stem with floral tape 5" (12.5 cm) below the base of the first flower (**G**). To hide where 2 stems meet (called a joint), attach a leaf on each side (**H**). Next, place the second bloom slightly lower than the first, and attach it with floral tape 2" (5 cm) below the bud stem (**I**).

Shape the main stem by bending it into a gentle curve. Angle the blooms for a final shaping. Using wire cutters, trim the stem to the desired length. Turn the flower upside down and tape the cut stem end with floral tape to finish.

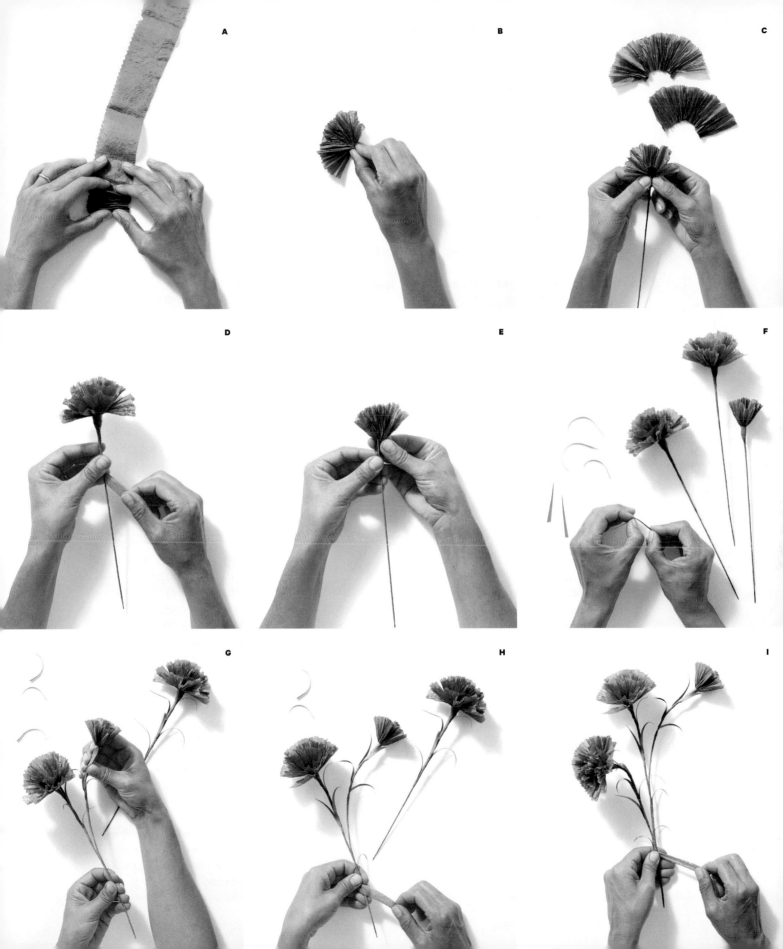

COSMOS

To me, these wild blooms represent a truly happy flower. They have a delicacy and lightness, and they are one of the few flowers that I construct entirely out of crepe paper. When I'm creating an arrangement, I place cosmos so that the blooms poke out the top. Their pretty, organic shape adds lots of movement to the overall mix. Plus, they are quick and easy to make! The most complicated part is the stylized leaf, which may take some practice to cut quickly.

GENERAL MATERIALS

• Scissors
• Fringing shears (optional)
• Green floral tape
• Wire cutters

FOR PETALS

• One 20" x 60" (51 x 152 cm) piece fuchsia fine crepe paper, dip-dyed with bleach (see page 16)

FOR MEDIUM POM-POM CENTERS

• Three 1" x 12" (2.5 x 30.5 cm) strips peach/yellow Doublette crepe paper
• Three 18" (46 cm) lengths 18-gauge pretaped wire

FOR BUD

• 1" x 3" (2.5 x 7.5 cm) strip fuchsia crepe paper, dip-dyed with water (see page 16)

FOR LEAVES

• 19" x 25" (48 x 63.5 cm) sheet green Canson paper
• Hot glue gun
• Hot glue sticks
• Five 9" (23 cm) lengths 24-gauge pretaped wire
• Five ½" x 2" (12 mm x 5 cm) pieces light-green tissue paper

COSMOS

FINISHED SIZE

Approximately 18" (46 cm)

1

PREPARE MATERIALS

Photocopy or trace the Cosmos Petal template on page 171 and cut out the petal shape. Cut twelve 3" x 12" (7.5 x 30.5 cm) pieces from the fuchsia fine crepe paper strip. Place the petal template on one piece so the top edge of the petal is at the bleach-dipped edge of the paper. Trace the template onto the crepe paper and cut out the petal shape. Repeat with the remaining crepe paper pieces to make a total of 12 petals. Because you are using crepe paper, you must cut out each petal individually.

Construct 3 medium pom-pom centers following the instructions on page 22, substituting crepe for tissue paper. You will use one center for the bud.

Photocopy or trace the Cosmos Leaf templates on page 171 and cut out the shapes. Trace 3 small and 2 large leaf templates onto the green Canson paper and cut them out.

Assemble the leaf stems following the instructions on page 27.

2

CREATE BLOOMS

Working on a smooth, low-friction surface, gently pinch the bottom edge of one petal with your fingertips (**A**). Place the pinched end of the petal on one of the pom-pom center stems, just below the center. Using floral tape, attach the petal to the stem, making sure the petal occupies no more than one-fifth of the space around the stem, and wrap the tape down and around the stem to about 1" (2.5 cm) below the base of the petal (**B**). The top edge of the first once-around of tape is your tapeline. As you attach each petal, you will start here.

Position a second petal overlapping the edge of the first by ⅕" (5 mm) and attach it with floral tape as you did for the first petal. Repeat with the remaining 4 petals, filling in the remaining space around the stem (**C**).

Repeat the process to create 1 more bloom. Since this is a branch with a few blooms, it's nice to have some diversity in their appearance. Try creating one that appears more open than the other. You might also consider creating a bloom with double the number of petals if you have enough supplies.

3

CONSTRUCT BUD

Wrap the 1" x 3" (2.5 x 7.5 cm) piece of fuchsia crepe paper around the pom-pom center with the bleach-dipped edge facing up, making sure that the paper is ⅛" (3 mm) above the top of the bud. With the center nicely encircled with crepe paper, pinch the crepe paper at the base of the bud and attach it to the wire with floral tape (**D**).

4

ASSEMBLE BRANCH

Start assembling the upper portion of the branch, which will consist of your largest, "lead" bloom, the bud, and 2 small leaves. Bend a small leaf at a 60-degree angle and attach it to the lead bloom about 2" to 3" (5 to 7.5 cm) below the bloom's base with floral tape (**E**). Repeat for the bud, attaching a small leaf 2" to 3" (5 to 7.5 cm) below the stem's base. Bend the last small leaf at a 60-degree angle and attach it to the final bloom about 2" to 3" (5 to 7.5 cm) below the bloom's base. Bend the bud's stem at a 60-degree angle 2" (5 cm) below the leaf. Using floral tape, attach the bud stem to the lead bloom stem 3" (7.5 cm) below the leaf to create the main stem (**G**). Next, attach one large leaf stem 1" (2.5 cm) below the joint (**H**).

Bend the final bloom 1½" (4 cm) below its leaf, and attach it to the main stem 2" (5 cm) below the large leaf. At 1" (2.5 cm) below that juncture, add the remaining large leaf on the left. Attach to the main stem 2" (5 cm) below the first joint (**I**).

Using wire cutters, trim the flower stem to 4" (10 cm) below the lowest leaf. Turn the flower upside down and wrap the cut stem end with floral tape to finish.

Position the flowers and bend the stems slightly so that they face you.

09
DESERT ROSE

The desert rose could be the star of any arrangement, although
I rarely use just one. The flower is delicate and versatile—
I like to make several in a range of colors, so that I can showcase
the vibrant blossoms from bright to faded. The real design
challenge is the leaf because it's complex, yet its shape provides
such a nice visual contrast to the blossom itself.

GENERAL MATERIALS

- Scissors
- Green floral tape
- Wire cutters

FOR PETALS

- Six 3" x 20"
  (7.5 x 50 cm) strips
  sunset tissue paper,
  dip-dyed with bleach
  (see page 16)

FOR POPPY CENTERS

- 3 safety cotton swabs
- 20" x 30" (50 x 76 cm)
  sheet light yellow tissue
  paper
- 20" x 60" (50 x 152
  cm) sheet light yellow
  Doublette crepe paper
- Three 9" (23 cm)
  lengths 18-gauge
  pretaped wire

FOR LEAVES

- 19" x 25" (48 x 63.5 cm)
  sheet green Canson
  paper
- Hot glue gun
- Hot glue sticks
- Six 9" (23 cm) lengths
  18-gauge pretaped wire
- Six ½" x 2"
  (12 mm x 5 cm) pieces
  light-green tissue paper

DESERT ROSE

FINISHED SIZE
Approximately 17" (43 cm)

PREPARE MATERIALS

Photocopy or trace the Desert Rose Petal template on page 168, and cut out the petal shape. Cut sixty 2" x 3" (5 x 7.5 cm) pieces from the sunset tissue strips. Divide the pieces into 6 stacks of 10 pieces each. Place the petal template on 1 stack, with the top of the petal at the bleached edge of the paper. Trace the template onto the tissue and cut it out to make 10 petals. Repeat with the remaining stacks to make a total of 60 petals.

Construct 3 poppy centers following the instructions on page 22.

Photocopy or trace the Desert Rose Leaf template on page 168 and cut out the shape. Trace 6 leaves onto the green Canson paper and cut them out. Assemble the leaf stems following the instructions on page 27.

CREATE PETALS

To give the petals a cupped shape, add a dart (see page 25) to each one (**A**). The 3-point fold for the dart should extend from the bottom of the petal to ½" (12 mm) from the top. The base of the dart fold should measure about ¼" (6 mm) and taper to a point. Repeat with the remaining petals, creating a total of 60 petals. Gently pinch the base of each petal to give it a cupped appearance (**B**).

ASSEMBLE BLOOMS

Place the pinched end of one petal at the base of a poppy center. Using as little tape as possible, attach the pinched end to the center stem, wrapping the tape down and around the wire twice, to about ½" (12 mm) below the petal base (**C**). Place a second petal alongside the first, overlapping their edges by ½" (12 mm). Attach it to the base with floral tape. Repeat with the remaining petals, overlapping the petal edges and encircling the center (**D**). Once you are comfortable, you can add 2 or 3 petals at a time. I prefer a more random placement of petals for this bloom. You will use 20 petals per bloom. Repeat to create 2 more blooms and fluff the petals (**E**).

ASSEMBLE STEM

Designate a top bloom, which is usually the smallest or most closed bloom—this will become your main stem. Place 2 leaf stems flush with the main stem and position them next to each other with the leaves directly below the flower base and extending ½" (12 mm) beyond the outer petals. Tack (see page 20) the leaf stems into place with floral tape. Wrap the tape to about 4" (10 cm) below the base of the leaves (**F**). Bend the stem forward at a 30-degree angle—about ½" (12 mm) below the base of the bloom—and adjust the leaves so that they are just kissing the edges of the petals, not pressed tightly up against them.

Bend the third leaf at a 30-degree angle, and attach it to the main stem 2" to 3" (5 to 7.5 cm) below the base of the first 2 leaves, opposite the second leaf. Bend the fourth leaf at a 30-degree angle and attach it 1½" (4 cm) down the stem, opposite the third (**G**). Attach the second bloom ½" (12 mm) below the fourth leaf. Attach the remaining bloom 2" (5 cm) below the second bloom. Bend each stem foward at a 30-degree angle about ½" (12 mm) below the base. Add the 2 remaining leaves to the left of the bloom to vary the layout a bit (**H**).

Using wire cutters, trim the flower stem to 4" (10 cm) below the last leaf. Turn the flower upside down and wrap the cut end with floral tape to finish. With your fingers, shape the main stem into a gentle S-curve to give it a more natural look (**I**).

A

B

C

D

E

F

G

H

I

10
HELLEBORE

Hellebores adore my yard (hello dry shade!), so I plant them everywhere. At first glance, they seem like such understated blooms, but when you look closely, you can see the complexity and beautiful subtleties between the varieties. Plus, they not only survive, but actually continue to blossom in the snow, which is unbelievably cool! The plant goes through several changes during its life span: The blooms start out a beautiful white, butter yellow, soft pink, or burgundy, lasting up to 2 months. Then the stamens fall off and the flowers turn green and leathery, like a seed pod. The following instructions show you how to make the mature version of the flower, but I recommend you try making them in all 3 colors—white, deep burgundy, and handpainted green—to explore and enjoy the different stages.

GENERAL MATERIALS

- Scissors
- Green floral tape
- Two 18" (46 cm) lengths 18-gauge reinforcement wire
- Wire cutters

FOR PETALS

- Four 3" x 20" (7.5 x 50 cm) strips burgundy tissue paper, dip-dyed with water (see page 16)

FOR COMPLEX STAMEN CENTERS

- 6 double-headed yellow stamen filaments
- Two 18" (46 cm) lengths 18-gauge pretaped wire
- Two 1" x 5" (2.5 x 13 cm) strips yellow Doublette crepe paper
- Two 2" x 11" (5 x 28 cm) strips soft green tissue paper

FOR LEAVES

- 19" x 25" (48 x 63.5 cm) sheet green Canson paper
- Hot glue gun
- Hot glue sticks
- Three 18" (46 cm) lengths 18-gauge pretaped wire
- Three ½" x 2" (12 mm x 5 cm) pieces light-green tissue paper

HELLEBORE

FINISHED SIZE
Approximately 12" (30.5 cm)

PREPARE MATERIALS

Photocopy or trace the Hellebore Petal template on page 163, and cut out the petal shapes. Cut thirty-two 2" x 3" (5 x 7.5 cm) pieces from the burgundy tissue strips. Divide the pieces into 4 stacks of 8 pieces each. Place the petal template on 1 stack, with the top of the petal at the water-dipped edge of the paper. Trace the template onto the tissue and cut it out to make 8 petals. Repeat with the remaining stacks to make a total of 32 petals.

Construct 2 complex stamen centers following the instructions on page 23.

Photocopy or trace the Hellebore Leaf template on page 163 and cut out the shape. Trace 5 leaves onto the green Canson paper and cut them out. Assemble the leaf stems following the instructions on page 27. Photocopy or trace the Hellebore Sepal template on page 163 and cut out the shape. Trace 2 sepals onto the green Canson paper and cut them out.

CREATE DOUBLE-PETALS

Place one petal on top of another to make a double-petal. To give the double-petals a cupped shape, add a dart (see page 25) (**A**). The 3-point fold for the dart should extend from the bottom of the petals to ½" (12 mm) from the top. The base of the dart fold should measure about ¼" (6 mm) and taper to a point. Repeat with the remaining petals, creating a total of 16 double-petals. Gently pinch the base of each double-petal to give it a cupped appearance (**B**).

ASSEMBLE BLOOMS

Place the pinched end of one double-petal at the base of one of the centers. Using as little tape as possible, attach the pinched end to the center stem, wrapping the tape down and around the wire twice, to about ½" (12 mm) below the petal base (**C**). Place a second double-petal alongside the first, overlapping their edges by ½" (12 mm). You want to fit 4 double-petals equally spaced around the center to create the first layer (**D**). Repeat with 4 more double-petals, placing them in between the points of the other petals, overlapping the petal edges and encircling the center. Fluff the bloom slightly and bend the stem forward at a 30-degree angle about ½" (12 mm) below the base of the bloom. Repeat this process to create 1 more bloom.

ASSEMBLE THE STEM

Fit 1 sepal leaf to the base of each bloom by sticking the stem through the center of the leaf. Press it in place with your fingers and tape the flanges to the stem (**E**). Hold the 2 blooms at the same height and lay the stems flush against each other. Tape the stems 5" (13 cm) down from where the blooms are bent. After they are taped together, separate them slightly and position them so that the 2 flower heads face in opposite directions. Bend each of the 3 leaves 60 degrees 3" (7.5 cm) below the base of each leaf. One at a time, lay each leaf stem flush to the main stem, and tape in place along the tape seam (**F–H**). Using wire cutters, trim the stem to 4" (10 cm). Turn flower upside down and wrap the cut stem end with floral tape to finish. Arrange the flowers in a pleasing manner (**I**).

A   B   C

D   E   F

G   H   I

12
CAMPANULA

I'm a total sucker for anything bell-shaped. When I was young, I had a wonderful children's book that was filled with illustrations of fairies and a garden, and what I remember best were all the campanulas! I grow them in my garden now, and since they propagate so easily, they are everywhere. They're also fun to make in paper form—I love how easy it is to play with size and quantity of blooms. Feel free to experiment!

GENERAL MATERIALS

- Scissors
- Green floral tape
- Wire cutters

FOR FLORETS AND SEPALS

- Four 3" x 20" (7.5 x 50 cm) strips lavender tissue paper, dip-dyed with bleach (see page 16), for florets
- Two 3" x 20" (7.5 x 50 cm) strips light-green tissue paper, for sepals

FOR SIMPLE STAMEN CENTERS

- 12 double-headed yellow stamen filaments
- Twelve 18" (46 cm) lengths 20-gauge pretaped wire

FOR BUDS

- Five 2" x 3" (5 x 7.5 cm) squares lavender tissue paper, dip-dyed with bleach (see page 16)
- Five 18" (46 cm) lengths 20-gauge pretaped wire

FOR LEAVES

- 19" x 25" (48 x 63.5 cm) sheet green Canson paper
- Hot glue gun
- Hot glue sticks
- Six 9" (23 cm) lengths 18-gauge pretaped wire
- Six ½" x 2" (12 mm x 5 cm) pieces light-green tissue paper

CAMPANULA

FINISHED SIZE
Approximately 21" (53 cm)

1

PREPARE MATERIALS

Photocopy or trace the Campanula Petal template on page 167 and cut out the petal shape. Cut the lavender petal tissue strips into twelve 3" x 5" (7.5 x 13 cm) pieces. Divide the tissue pieces into 2 stacks of 6. Trace the template onto the top piece of tissue and cut out the petal shape to make 12 connected petals.

Photocopy or trace the Campanula Sepal template on page 167 and cut out the sepal shapes. Cut the light-green sepal tissue strips into twelve 2" x 3" (5 x 7.5 cm) pieces. Trace the template onto the tissue and cut out the sepal shape to make 12 connected sepals.

Construct 12 simple stamen centers following the instructions on page 23.

Photocopy or trace the Campanula Leaf templates on page 167 and cut out the leaf shapes. Trace 2 small and 4 large leaf shapes onto the green Canson paper and cut them out. Assemble the leaf stems following the instructions on page 23.

2

SHAPE CONNECTED PETALS

Working on a smooth, low-friction surface, gently gather the bottom edge of a connected petal into a fanlike shape with your fingertips (**A**). Position the connected petal about 1" (2.5 cm) from the top of one of the simple stamen center stems so the stamens are even with the petal edges but visible when the flower is viewed from the side (**B**). Adjust the petals so that they are evenly spaced and overlap slightly at their bases. Attach the connected petal with floral tape, wrapping down and around the stem to about 1" (2.5 cm) below the base of the petal (**C**). Shape the bloom by inserting your fingertip inside the flower. Gently expand and smooth the gathered base of the connected petal between the round tip of your index finger and your thumb. Repeat with the remaining florets to create a total of 12.

3

ATTACH SEPALS

Working on a smooth, low-friction surface, gently gather the bottom edge of a connected sepal into a fanlike shape with your fingertips and press it to the base of the bloom (**D**). Attach with floral tape to create the sepal (**E**). Repeat with the remaining sepals.

4

CONSTRUCT BUDS

Roll one lavender tissue square into a tight tube (**F+G**). Twist the top half tightly (**H**). Gather the bottom edge and attach it to a pretaped wire using floral tape (**I**). Repeat with the remaining squares to create a total of 5 buds.

5

ASSEMBLE STEM

Bend 1 bud and 1 bloom at a 60-degree angle 1" (2.5 cm) below the base. Attach them to a second bloom at the point where the stems are bent (**J**). This creates a cluster of 2 blooms and a bud. Wrap the tape down and around the stems to about 1" (2.5 cm) below the base and add the next 3 blooms, each bent at a 60-degree angle, 1" (2.5 cm) lower on the stem (**K**). Bend 3 blooms and two buds at a 60-degree angle 1" (2.5 cm) from their bases and attach them to the stem 2" (5 cm) below the previous cluster. Adjust them in a pleasing manner around the blooms. You can arrange blooms and buds to your liking. I then added a 4-bloom 2-bud cluster (**L**). Bend each bloom down to point toward the floor (**M**).

6

ATTACH LEAVES

Bend the leaf stems at a 60-degree angle 3" (7.5 cm) from their base and position 3 large leaves and one small leaf 1½" (4 cm) below the last row of blooms or buds on the main stem. Attach them with floral tape (**N+O**). Repeat to form a second row (**P**). Using wire cutters, trim the stem to 8" (20 cm) below the last row of leaves. Turn the flower upside down and wrap the cut stem end with floral tape to finish.

13.

PEEGEE HYDRANGEA

I grew up in California and never realized how much the seasons
impacted what I know about flowers until I moved to
New York. Take the peegee hydrangea, a rare fall bloom. Its unique
white, poufy clouds of flowers unify my yard as the leaves are
falling. The peegee begins as a lime-green bushel of flowers,
then moves to white, before turning a pinkish tone and finally back
to a deeper green. I love their romantic, lush, and abundant
cone shape and long, arching branches. As a bonus, if you make
this exact flower with lavender tissue and yellow stamens,
it becomes a lilac!

GENERAL MATERIALS

- Scissors
- Green floral tape
- Wire cutters

FOR PETALS

- Three 3" x 20"
  (7.5 x 50 cm) strips
  light-green tissue paper,
  dip-dyed with water
  (see page 16)
- Three 3" x 20"
  (7.5 x 50 cm) strips soft
  pink tissue paper,
  dip-dyped with water
  (see page 16)

FOR SIMPLE STAMEN CENTERS

- 30 double-headed
  gray-with-white-tip
  stamen filaments
- Thirty 9" (23 cm)
  lengths 20-gauge wire,
  pretaped with green
  floral tape

FOR LEAVES

- 19" x 25" (48 x 63.5 cm)
  sheet green Canson
  paper
- Hot glue gun
- Hot glue sticks
- Five 9" (23 cm) lengths
  18-gauge pretaped wire
- Five ½" x 2"
  (12 mm x 5 cm) pieces
  light-green tissue paper

PEEGEE HYDRANGEA

FINISHED SIZE
Approximately 13" (33 cm)

1

PREPARE MATERIALS

Photocopy or trace the Peegee Hydrangea Petal template on page 162 and cut out the connected petal shape. Cut fifteen 3" x 3" (7.5 x 7.5 cm) pieces from each of the light-green tissue paper strips and the soft pink tissue paper strips and stack them into 3 groups of 10 pieces each. Trace the template onto the tissue and cut it out to make 30 connected petals.

Create 30 simple stamen centers (see page 23). Tape the stamen flush to the top of the wire each time.

Photocopy or trace the Peegee Hydrangea Leaf template on page 162 and cut out the leaf shape. Trace 5 leaves onto the green Canson paper and cut them out. Assemble the leaf stems following the instructions on page 27.

2

CREATE FLORETS

Working on a smooth, low-friction surface, gently gather the bottom edge of a connected petal into a fanlike shape with your fingertips (**A**). Position the connected petal flush with the stamen center so that you don't see any of the actual wire, just the stamen (**B**). Adjust the petal ends so that they are evenly spaced and overlap slightly at their base. Attach the connected petal with floral tape (**C**). Repeat with the remaining 29 petals to create a total of 30 florets. Bend each stem 15 degrees 1" (2.5 cm) below the base of each floret.

3

ASSEMBLE BLOOM

Tack (see page 20) 3 pink florets together with floral tape at the point where each is bent. Wrap the tape straight down and around the stems about 2" (5 cm) (**D**). Continue adding rows of florets in ¼" (6 mm) increments working down the stem, transitioning from pink to green flowers, positioning them as you go to create a half-cone shape (**E–G**). At the top of the stem, each row is 3 florets across, and at the bottom each row is 5 to 6 florets across. During the process, trim the stems at varying lengths in order to reduce the bulk of the main stem. When your cone is completed, gently bend the main stem halfway up to create a slight arc and reposition the florets accordingly (**H**).

4

ASSEMBLE STEM

Take 2 leaves and attach them 1" (2.5 cm) down the stem to frame the back and sides of the flower (**I**). Tape 2 more leaves together to create a small branch, and attach it to the right side of the bloom 1" (2.5 cm) below the first 2 leaves. Add one more leaf to cover the branch. Using wire cutters, trim the flower stem to 5" (13 cm) below the lowest leaf. Turn the flower upside down and wrap the cut stem end with floral tape to finish.

14
BEARDED IRIS

My mother grew bearded irises when I was growing up.
They were some of the few fancy flowers in her garden, and I have
always been fascinated by their unusual form. The Bearded Iris
is so delicate yet so resilient. The petals have an iridescent
quality that I could stare at all day. It took me a while to figure out
how to create them in paper but I'm so happy with the result,
and I hope you will be, too.

GENERAL MATERIALS

- Scissors
- Fringing shears (optional)
- Hot glue gun
- Hot glue sticks
- Five 18" (46 cm) lengths 18-gauge reinforcement wire
- Wire cutters

FOR PETALS

- Two 4" x 20" (10 x 50 cm) strips lavender tissue paper, dip-dyed with magenta and blue dye (see page 16)
- Six 9" (23 cm) lengths 18-gauge white pretaped wire

FOR FRILL

- Two 2" x 8" (5 x 20 cm) pieces lavender tissue paper
- 3½" x 6" (9 x 15 cm) strip orange fine crepe paper

FOR BUD

- 4" x 20" (10 x 50 cm) strip lavender tissue paper, dip-dyed with magenta and blue dye (see page 16)
- 18" (46 cm) length 18-gauge pretaped wire
- 2" x 2" (5 x 5 cm) square light-green tissue paper

FOR LEAVES

- 19" x 25" (48 x 63.5 cm) sheet green Canson paper
- Six ½" x 5" (12 mm x 13 cm) pieces light-green tissue paper
- Six 9" (23 cm) lengths 20-gauge pretaped wire

BEARDED IRIS

FINISHED SIZE
Approximately 26" (66 cm)

1

PREPARE MATERIALS

Photocopy or trace the Bearded Iris Petal template on page 166 and cut out the petal shape. Cut twelve 3" x 4" (7.5 x 10 cm) pieces from the tissue paper strips and stack them. Place the template on the stack of tissue pieces so the top of the petal is positioned on the top edge of the paper. Trace the template onto the tissue and cut it out to make 12 petals.

The frill is comprised of two pieces: the lavender tissue and the orange crepe paper. Use scissors or fringing shears to create a 1" (2.5 cm) fringe along the top edge of the two 2" x 8" (5 x 20 cm) pieces of lavender tissue paper intended for the frill. Set them aside

Cut the orange fine crepe paper into three 2" x 3½" (5 x 9 cm) pieces, making sure that the grain runs lengthwise, or parallel to the longer side of the rectangle (see page 14). Photocopy or trace the Bearded Iris Frill template on page 166 and cut out the frill petal shape. Trace the template onto the orange fine crepe paper pieces and cut them out. Cut a ½" (12 mm) fringe along the outer edge of the petals with regular scissors.

Photocopy or trace the Bearded Iris Leaf templates on page 166 and cut out the leaf shapes. Trace an assortment of 5 leaves onto the green Canson paper and cut them out. Assemble the leaf stems following the instructions on page 27. Glue the wire to the crease rather than the underside of the leaf, and place the wire in the center and about 2½" (5 cm) from the bottom edge as shown in the photo on page 79.

Photocopy or trace the Bearded Iris Bud Leaf Casing template on page 166 and cut out the casing shapes. Trace the casing onto the 2" x 2" (5 x 5 cm) square light-green tissue paper and cut it out.

2

CREATE DOUBLE-PETALS

To create the double-petals, place a petal on a flat surface and use a hot glue gun to glue the wire so that when placed along the length of the petal, the end of the wire is ¼" (6 mm) from the top of the petal (**A**). Glue another petal on top of the first, bottom edges aligned, so that the 2 petals sandwich the wire. Repeat with remaining petals, glue, and wire to create a total of 6 double-petal stems.

3

CREATE BLOOMS

Three double-petals will make up the top part, or "crown," of the flower. Shape the petals by pinching the tissue at each base and bending the wire inside each double-petal stem at 2 subsequent right angles, resembling a stairstep (**B+C**). Tape one double-petal stem to another by placing them together to form two right angles and wrapping the stems in floral tape 2" (5 cm) down the stem (**D**). Add the third double-petal stem, taping it to the other 2 in the same fashion (**E**). Adjust the spacing and shape so that the petals create a cupped form (**F**).

Working on a smooth, low-friction surface, gently gather the lavender tissue frill strip into a fanlike shape with your fingertips (**G**). Press the pinched end in place, covering half of the base (**H+I**). Attach it to the stem below the cupped form base with floral tape. Repeat with the remaining piece of lavender frill to cover the other half of the stem (**J**).

Shape the orange frills. Give each one a gentle curl with the outer edge of your scissors (see page 25) and separate the fringe by slowly pulling the frill through your thumb and pointer finger. Each one of these 3 pieces corresponds to each of the 3 remaining double-petal stems.

A

Bend the wire at the base of each of the remaining double-petal stems to a 45-degree angle. Position a frill in the center of one petal, pinch the crepe paper at the base of the fringe, and tape it to the cupped double-petal base (**K**). Repeat with remaining 2 frills and double-petal stems. Each bottom petal should line up with a top petal. Bend the double-petals at a downward angle (**L**). Add 2 reinforcement wires to elongate the flower stem.

CREATE BUD

Take your strip of dyed lavender 4" x 20" (10 x 50 cm) tissue and fold it into thirds lengthwise. Roll the tissue into a loose tube, about 1" (2.5 cm) in diameter (**M**). Pinch and gather it at the bottom and attach it to the pretaped wire with floral tape. Twist the top edge (**N**). Wrap the casing tissue paper around the base of the bud and tape. Attach a leaf to the bud stem 6" (15 cm) below the base of the bud (**O**).

ASSEMBLE STEM

Place one of the leaf stems flush against the main bloom stem 6" (15 cm) below the main bloom. Attach the leaf stem to the main stem with floral tape, wrapping until you reach the end of the flower-stem wire.

Attach one 18" (46 cm) reinforcement wire to the main stem by inserting the top of the wire into the base of the stem and laying it flush alongside the existing stem wires. (You will see a gap that was created where the leaf stem wire and main stem were taped together. Tuck the top end of the reinforcement wire into the gap.) Secure it with floral tape, wrapping the tape the full length of the stem.

Attach the next leaf about 3" (7.5 cm) below the base of the first leaf.

Add another reinforcement wire to the stem as you did with the previous one, and then attach the bud stem 2" (5 cm) below the leaf attached to the bud stem, and 4" (10 cm) below the leaf attached to the flower stem. Next add a leaf 1" (2.5 cm) below the flower leaf (**P**).

Using wire cutters, trim the flower stem to 4" (10 cm) below the lowest leaf. Turn the flower upside down and wrap the cut stem end with floral tape to finish.

B

C

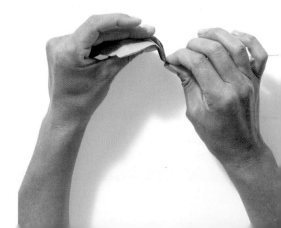

G

P

K

O

15.

CYCLAMEN

I was approached by Tiffany & Co. to design a paper flower for the holiday display in their flagship store in New York City, and their only request was "anything but poinsettia." What resulted was an ethereal display of cyclamen—dozens of fluffy, fairy-winged flowers floating above their plants. As far as technique goes, no other flower has a petal that is made like this. Try your hand at making a few of these simple, but unusual, little flowers.

GENERAL MATERIALS

- Scissors
- Green floral tape
- Wire cutters

FOR PETALS

- Two 4" x 20" (10 x 50 cm) strips soft pink tissue paper, dip-dyed with orange dye (see page 16)

FOR SIMPLE STAMEN CENTER

- 3 double-headed yellow stamen filaments
- Three 9" (23 cm) lengths 20-gauge pretaped wire

FOR BUDS

- 2 mini cotton swabs (see page 12)
- Four 2" x 2" (5 x 5 cm) squares soft pink tissue paper, dip-dyed with orange dye (see page 16)
- Two 18" (46 cm) lengths 20-gauge pretaped wire

FOR LEAVES

- 19" x 25" (48 x 63.5 cm) sheet green Canson paper
- Paintbrush
- Gouache paint
- Hot glue gun
- Hot glue sticks
- Five 9" (23 cm) lengths 18-gauge pretaped wire
- Five ½" x 2" (12 mm x 5 cm) pieces light-green tissue paper

CYCLAMEN

FINISHED SIZE
Approximately 14" (35.5 cm)

(1)

PREPARE MATERIALS

Photocopy or trace the Cyclamen Petal template on page 172 and cut out the petal shape. Cut six 4" x 4" (10 x 10 cm) pieces from the 4" x 20" (10 x 50 cm) petal tissue paper strips and stack them. Place the petal template on the stack of 6 so the top of the petal is at the pink edge of the paper. Trace the template onto the tissue and cut it out to make 6 petals.

Construct 3 mini cotton swab buds following the Poppy Center instructions on page 22.

Construct 5 simple stamen centers on 9" (23 cm) wires following the instructions on page 23.

Photocopy or trace the Cyclamen Leaf templates on page 172 and cut out the leaf shape. Trace 5 leaves onto the green Canson paper and cut them out. Paint the center of the leaves following the instructions on page 17, then fold them and assemble the leaf stems following the instructions on page 27.

(2)

CREATE DOUBLE-PETALS

Place one petal directly on top of another to make a double-petal. Fold the bottom edge up ¼" (6 mm) (**A**). Trim the extra paper from the 2 corners to minimize the paper when the flower is folded.

(3)

CONSTRUCT BLOOMS

Take one of the simple stamen stem, and bend the wire 1" (2.5 cm) below the stamen tip by wrapping it around your finger (**B**). Hold the wire against one double-petal so that the stamen just peeks out below the fold in the center of the petal

(**C**). Fold the double-petal in half around the wire (**D**). Holding it firmly in place on the wire, gather the 2 ends of the tissue paper toward the stem, and tape in place (**E+F**). Separate the petals and fluff them. Repeat to create 2 more blooms.

(4)

ASSEMBLE THE STEM

Add the buds to the center of the arrangement. Bend the 2 buds downward and around your finger ½" (12 mm) from the tapeline (**G**). Bend a bloom stem at a 90-degree angle ½" (12 mm) below the tapeline, and 1" (2.5 cm) below that, bend the stem at a 90-degree angle in the opposite direction (**H**). Repeat for each bloom.

(5)

ASSEMBLE THE CLUSTER

Make a pleasing cluster of blooms and tape them together at heights from 7" (18 cm) to 4" (10 cm) from the last bend in the stem so that they radiate from the center of the plant. Tape down to the end of the stem.

(6)

ATTACH LEAVES

Surround the cluster with leaves. Bend the 5 leaves at a 90-degree angle from the leaf to the stem. Position the leaves around and below the blooms, then bend the leaf stems at a 15-degree angle from the cluster (**I**). Attach with floral tape. Using wire cutters, trim the flower to the desired length. Turn flower upside down and wrap the cut stem end with floral tape to finish.

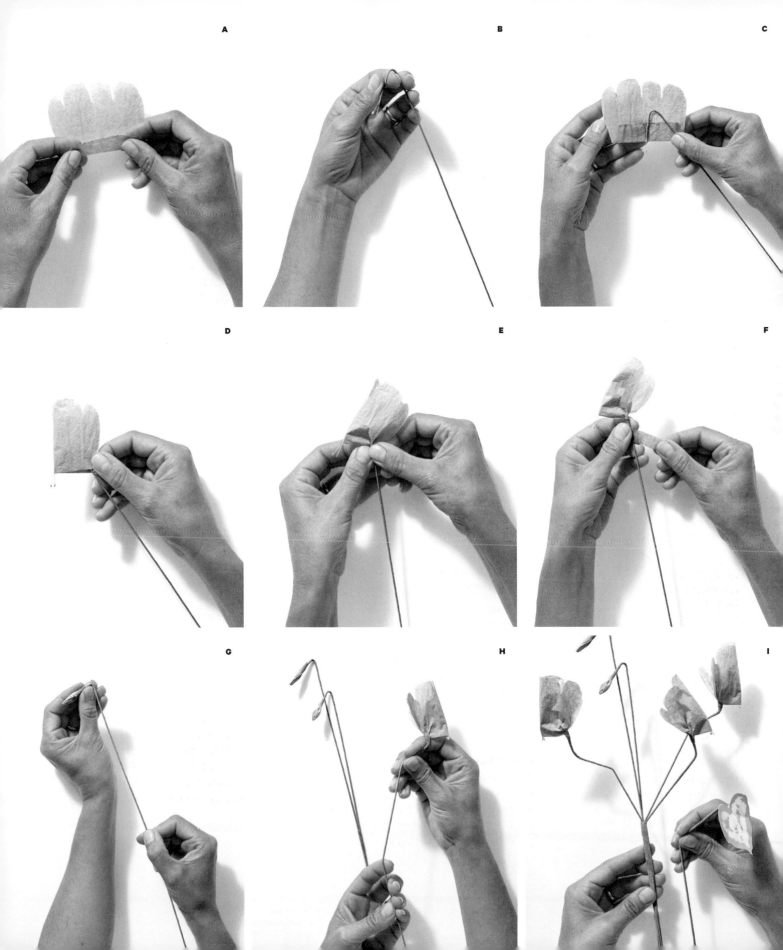

16·
CROCU'S

Many don't know that the dried stigma of the crocus stamen is what's known as saffron, the spice. As the first flower to open in spring after the long winter, the crocus is a welcome sight. They are beautiful in white, but I really love the purple-striped variety, and these variegated petals are super easy to re-create in paper.

GENERAL MATERIALS

- Scissors
- Green floral tape
- Fringing shears (optional)
- Wire cutters

FOR PETALS

- Four 3" x 20" (7.5 x 50 cm) strips cream tissue paper, dip-dyed yellow and orange (see page 16)

FOR SMALL POM-POM CENTER

- 20" x 60" (50 x 152 cm) sheet soft yellow fine crepe paper
- 9" (23 cm) length 20-gauge pretaped wire
- 2" x 3" (5 x 7.5 cm) strip orange and yellow Doublette crepe paper

FOR LEAVES

- 19" x 25" (48 x 63.5 cm) sheet green Canson paper

CROCUS

FINISHED SIZE
Approximately 16" (40.5 cm)

1

PREPARE MATERIALS

Photocopy or trace the Crocus Petal template on page 172 and cut out the petal shape. Cut the petal tissue strips into twenty-four 3" x 2" (7.5 x 5 cm) pieces. Trace the template onto the tissue and cut out the petal shape. Orient the tissue piece so that the cream edge is on top. Repeat with the remaining pieces to make a total of 24 petals.

Construct a small pom-pom center with the yellow fine crepe paper, following the instructions on page 22. Photocopy or trace the Crocus Filament template on page 172 and cut out the filament shapes. Trace 3 filaments onto the orange Doublette crepe paper and cut them out. Pull each one lenghwise between your thumb and index finger to shape it, and attach them evenly around the center with floral tape (**A+B**).

Photocopy or trace the Crocus Leaf templates on page 172 and cut out the leaf shapes. Trace 4 leaves onto the green Canson paper and cut them out.

2

CREATE DOUBLE-PETALS

Place one petal on top of another to make a double-petal. To give the double-petals a cupped shape, add a shallow dart (see page 25) (**C**). The 3-point fold for the dart should extend from the bottom of the petals to 1½" (4 cm) from the top. The base of the dart fold should measure about ¼" (6 mm) across and taper to a point. Gently gather the base of each double-petal to give it a cupped shape. Repeat with the remaining petals to make a total of 12 double-petals.

3

CONSTRUCT BLOOM

Place the pinched end of one double-petal at the base of the pom-pom center. Using as little tape as possible, attach the pinched end to the center stem with floral tape, wrapping the tape down and around the wire twice, to about ½" (12 mm) below the petal base (**D**). The top edge of your first piece of tape is now your tapeline. Place a second double-petal alongside the first, overlapping their edges by ½" (12 mm). Continue with the next 2 petals, but be mindful of your placement—you want to be able to fit the first 4 double-petals equally spaced around the center to create your first layer (**E**). Repeat the process with 4 more double-petals, evenly spacing them in between the points of the other petals, overlapping the petal edges and encircling the center (**F**). Finally, repeat with the remaining 4 double-petals (you can omit this step if you prefer a smaller bloom). Fluff the bloom slightly and bend the stem forward at a 30-degree angle about ½" (12 mm) below the base of the bloom.

4

ASSEMBLE THE STEM

To shape the leaves, pull each one lengthwise between your thumb and index finger to create a gentle curl (**G**). Position a leaf at the base of the bloom (so the leaf touches the side of the bloom and curls back down to the stem). Pinch the bottom of the leaf against the stem wire, then attach the bottom ½" (12 mm) of the leaf to the stem with floral tape. Repeat with the remaining 3 leaves, attaching them down and around the stem at 1" (2.5 cm) intervals (**H**). Trim the flower stem to the desired length, then turn the flower upside down and wrap with floral tape to finish (**I**).

17

EASTER LILY

I loved the romance of the Ridley Scott movie *Legend*—the fairy-tale atmosphere of the setting is breathtaking, mainly due to the fields of Easter lilies. It's a stylist's dream job to create a set like that, and I have been intrigued by the challenge of bringing something like that to life ever since. The technique I came up with—using wire to give structure to long, dynamic petals of tissue—is one I use with the Bearded Iris (page 78), as well. It's a great solution to something I puzzled over for a long time.

GENERAL MATERIALS

- Scissors
- Fringing shears (optional)
- Green floral tape
- Hot glue gun
- Hot glue sticks
- Wire cutters
- Six 18" (46 cm) lengths 18-gauge reinforcement wire

FOR PETALS AND BUDS

- Three 9" x 20" (23 x 50 cm) strips light pink tissue paper, dip-dyed with bleach (see page 16)
- Seventeen 18" (46 cm) lengths 20-gauge white pretaped wire
- Yellow floral tape

FOR EASTER LILY CENTERS (CARPELS AND STAMENS)

- 12" x 1¼" (30.5 x 3 cm) strip orange Doublette crepe paper
- Eight 2" x 2" (5 x 5 cm) squares yellow tissue paper
- Fourteen 9" (23 cm) lengths 20-gauge yellow pretaped wire
- Yellow floral tape

FOR LEAVES

- 19" x 25" (48 x 63.5 cm) sheet green Canson paper
- Sixteen 9" (23 cm) lengths 20-gauge pretaped wire
- Sixteen ½" x 2" (12 mm x 5 cm) pieces light-green tissue paper

DIRECTIONS

EASTER LILY

FINISHED SIZE
Approximately 36" (91 cm)

PREPARE MATERIALS

Photocopy or trace the Easter Lily Petal template on page 168 and cut out the petal shape. Cut thirty-four 1¼" x 9" (3 x 23 cm) pieces from the strips of light pink tissue paper. Trace the petal template onto a stack of tissue paper and cut out the petal shape. Repeat to make a total of 34 petals.

Construct the Easter Lily carpels. To begin, stack two of the yellow tissue paper squares and fold them into a small square ⅛" x ⅛" (3 x 3 mm) Place it on top of a yellow pretaped wire. Take the 2 remaining yellow tissue paper squares, wrap them around the folded square, pinch the remaining paper to the wire underneath the square, and secure with yellow floral tape (**A+B**). Repeat to create a second carpel.

Construct the Easter Lily stamens. Cut the Doublette crepe paper strip into six 2" (5 cm) pieces. Roll each strip of crepe paper into a tight cylinder, secure with a small dot of glue from a glue gun, insert a 9" (23 cm) 20-gauge yellow pretaped wire into the base, and secure with yellow floral tape (**C**). Trim the tops of each of the 6 cylinders with scissors to round the edges (**D**). Surround the carpel with the 6 stamen wires so that the carpel is ½" (12 mm) above the stamens. Bend each at at a 45-degree angle at the base of the tape (**E**). Secure the wires together 2" (5 cm) below the bend of the stamen, and reposition each stamen so they appear to encircle and radiate from the carpel (**F**). Repeat to create a second set of stamens.

Photocopy or trace the Easter Lily Leaf templates on page 168 and cut out the leaf shapes. Trace an assortment of 16 leaves onto the green Canson paper and cut them out. Assemble the leaf stems following the instructions on page 27. Use the edge of a closed pair of scissors to curl 10 of the leaves, creating a gentle arc shape in the top 2" (5 cm) of the leaf.

CREATE DOUBLE-PETALS

Lay one petal flat on your work surface. Place one of the 20-gauge petal wires lengthwise in the center of the petal. Hot-glue the wire in place along the length of the petal, making sure the wire doesn't protrude over the top of the petal. Place another strip of hot glue on the other side of the wire, and lay a second petal on top so that the 2 petals sandwich the wire. Repeat 16 more times to create 17 double-petals (**G**).

ASSEMBLE BUD

Adjust and position 3 double-petal stems together to create a bud with 3 sides. Tape the double-petal stems together 2" (5 cm) down the stem with green floral tape. Bend the top 1" (2.5 cm) or so of each petal inward so that the bud is hollow on the inside but closed at the top (**H**). Tape 2 additional double-petal stems to the outside of the form where needed to fill in any gaps. Bend inward at the top as well.

ASSEMBLE BLOOMS

Pinch the base of one petal, and attach it and its stem to the lily center with green floral tape, wrapping the tape down and around the wire to about 2" (5 cm) below the base of the center. Repeat to attach 5 more petal stems, spacing them evenly around the base. Shape the petals so they curl outward from the lily center (**I**). Bend the petals upward around the center to create a tight cone shape. Then curl the top third of the petal tips outward to create a trumpet shape. This might take a series of small tweaks to get the shape just right (**J**). Repeat to create a second bloom.

ASSEMBLE STEM

Bend the bud 1" (2.5 cm) from its base at a 60-degree angle. Attach one curled leaf 1" (2.5 cm) down the stem from the bend. Bend one bloom stem at a 90-degree angle 1" (2.5 cm) below its base and attach it to the bud stem 3" (7.5 cm) below the curled leaf and 2" (5 cm) below the bend of the flower (**K**). Repeat the process to attach the second bloom 1" (2.5 cm) below the first bloom. Add 4 leaves opposite each other 1" (2.5 cm) below that seam (**L**).

Attach an 18" (46 cm) reinforcement wire to extend the stem by inserting the wire through the bottom of the stem where the other wires are loose. Secure it with green floral tape. Working down the stem every 2" (5 cm), add 4 more 4-leaf sets (**M**). With each leaf set, add a reinforcement wire. It does not matter which leaves you attach and in what order; I like to work randomly. Use your final reinforcement wire to create an even and consistent thickness to the bottom of the stem, attaching it through the bottom of the stem. Trim the stem 11" (28 cm) below your final leaf. Turn upside down and wrap the cut stem end with green floral tape. Adjust leaf position to lend balance to the stem.

18

NARCISSUS'S

There are so many types of narcissus, but this version is inspired by bulbs I found in San Francisco's Chinatown that boast chunkier, waxier, and more robust blooms. These flowers are interesting because they don't have to grow in the ground— you can "force" them in a water-and-gravel-filled dish. I've created my narcissus in yellow to be more striking than the usual white variety, and to set them apart from their smaller relative, paperwhites (page 100). These hugely popular flowers typically bloom in the spring, but in paper, they last forever.

GENERAL MATERIALS

• Scissors
• Green floral tape
• Wire cutters

FOR BLOOMS

• 3" x 20" (7.5 x 50 cm) strip yellow tissue paper, dip-dyed with bleach (see page 16)
• 3" x 20" (7.5 x 50 cm) strip burnt orange tissue paper, dip-dyed with bleach (see page 16)
• Five 9" (23 cm) lengths 20-gauge pretaped wire

FOR BUDS

• 2 safety cotton swabs
• Four 2" x 2" (5 x 5 cm) squares yellow tissue paper
• Two 9" (23 cm) lengths 20-gauge pretaped wire

FOR LEAVES

• 19" x 25" (48 x 63.5 cm) sheet green Canson paper
• Hot glue gun
• Hot glue sticks
• Seven 18" (46 cm) lengths 18-gauge pretaped wire
• Seven ½" x 2" (12 mm x 5 cm) pieces light-green tissue paper

NARCISSUS

FINISHED SIZE
Approximately 15" (38 cm)

PREPARE MATERIALS

Photocopy or trace the Narcissus Petal templates on page 171 and cut out the petal shape. Cut the yellow petal tissue strip into five 3" x 3" (7.5 x 7.5 cm) pieces. Trace the main petal template onto the tissue and cut out the petal shape to make 5 connected petals.

Cut the burnt orange tissue strip into five 3" x 4" (7.5 x 10 cm) pieces. Trace the Narcissus Center template onto the tissue and cut out the center petal shape to make 5 center petals.

Photocopy or trace the Paperwhite/Narcissus Leaf templates on page 171 and cut out the shapes. Trace any combination of 7 large and small leaves onto green Canson paper and cut them out. Assemble the leaves following the instructions on page 71.

CREATE BLOOMS

Place a center petal against your index finger with the scalloped edge oriented toward the base of your finger, positioned so the scalloped edge is 1" (2.5 cm) from the end of your index finger (**A**). Wrap the petal around your finger and, with your other hand, twist the paper overhanging your fingertip (**B**). Carefully remove the petal and tape the twisted end to an 18" (46 cm) pretaped wire, wrapping the wire to 1" (2.5 cm) below the base of the petal (**C**). Repeat with the remaining center petals to make a total of 5 centers.

Working on a smooth, low-friction surface, gently gather the bottom edge of one of the main connected petals into a fanlike shape with your fingertips (**D**). Position the connected petal directly under the center petal and adjust the petal ends so that they are evenly spaced and overlap slightly at their base (**E**). Tape into place.

ASSEMBLE BUDS

Trim one end of the cotton swab stick ⅓" (8 mm) from the bulb. Insert the pretaped wire into the hollow of the cotton swab stem and secure it with green floral tape, covering 3" to 4" (7.5 to 10 cm) down the wire. Place 2 squares of orange tissue paper on top of each other. Position the bulb of the cotton swab in the middle of the tissue squares and wrap them completely around the swab. Secure the tissue squares tightly around the base of the cotton swab with floral tape. Repeat 1 more time for a total of 2 buds.

ASSEMBLE BLOOM CLUSTER

Bend 1 bloom and 1 bud at a 60-degree angle 1½" (4 cm) from their bases. Place the second bud so its stem is flush with the bent stems and attach them with floral tape 1½" (4 cm) below where the stems are bent to create a bloom cluster (**F**). Wrap and wind the tape around the 3 stems. Continue adding blooms in this manner, adjusting spacing as necessary (**G**).

ATTACH LEAVES

Position 2 leaves of any size at the back of the flower about 5" (13 cm) below the base of the taped bloom stems and attach them with floral tape, wrapping 2" (5 cm) from the base of the leaves (**H**). Place 3 more leaves ½" (12 mm) below the first group of leaves, and attach the leaves to the main stem with floral tape, wrapping 2" (5 cm) down the stem. Position and attach the remaining 2 leaves to the stem ½" (12 mm) below the previous 3. Angle and position the leaves, bending them slightly at the base of each leaf (**I**). Using wire cutters, trim the main stem to 5" (13 cm) below the base of the leaves. Turn the flower upside down and wrap the cut stem end with floral tape to finish.

19.

PAPERWHITE

Paperwhites were the big thing when I first moved to New York. The florist I worked for would position the bulbs in pyramids so that they were stacked and grew into arrangements of different heights rather than growing flat in the pot. I love how they start so precise and end up so unruly—first they grow upright, then they flop over. And they thrive in the least expected conditions: They'll even grow in a paper bag under your bed!

GENERAL MATERIALS

- Scissors
- Green floral tape
- Wire cutters
- Pencil

FOR BLOOMS

- Two 3" x 20"
(7.5 x 50 cm) strips
white tissue paper

FOR SIMPLE STAMEN CENTERS

- 3" x 20" (7.5 x 50 cm)
strip white tissue paper
- 7 double-headed
yellow stamen filaments
- Seven 18" (46 cm)
lengths 20-gauge
pretaped wire

FOR BUDS

- 2 safety cotton swabs
- Four 2" x 2" (5 x 5 cm)
squares white tissue
paper
- Two 18" (46 cm)
lengths 18-gauge pre-
taped wire

FOR LEAVES

- 19" x 25" (48 x 63.5 cm)
sheet green Canson
paper
- Hot glue gun
- Hot glue sticks
- Seven 9" (23 cm)
lengths 18-gauge
pretaped wire
- Seven ½" x 2"
(12 mm x 5 cm) pieces
light-green tissue paper

PAPERWHITES

FINISHED SIZE
Approximately 15" (38 cm)

 1

PREPARE MATERIALS

Photocopy or trace the Paperwhite Petal template on page 171 and cut out the petal shape. Cut the petal tissue strip into seven 3" x 3" (7.5 x 7.5 cm) pieces and stack them. Trace the template onto the tissue and cut out the petal shape to make 7 connected petals.

Photocopy or trace the Paperwhite Center template on page 171 and cut out the center shape. Cut the center tissue strip into seven 2" x 3" (5 x 7.5 cm) pieces. Trace the template onto the tissue and cut out the petal shape to make 7 center pieces.

Create 7 simple stamen centers on 18" (46 cm) lengths of 20-gauge wire following the instructions on page 23.

Photocopy or trace the Paperwhite/Narcissus Leaf templates on page 171 and cut out the shapes. Trace 7 leaves in varying sizes onto green Canson paper and cut them out. Assemble the leaves following the instructions on page 27.

 2

CREATE BLOOMS

Hold a stamen in place on the blunt end of a standard pencil, with the head of the stamen pointing toward the point and ½" (12 mm) below the tip of the blunt end. Place a center petal over the stamen so the scalloped edge is ½" (12 mm) from the blunt end, positioned toward the point. Wrap the petal around the blunt end, encircling the stamen (**A**). Twist the paper end overhanging the blunt end (**B**). Carefully remove the bloom from the pencil and tape the twisted end of the bloom to a simple stamen center, wrapping the wire to 1" (2.5 cm) below the base of the bloom (**C**). Repeat with the remaining stamens and center petals to make a total of 7 bloom centers.

Working on a smooth, low-friction surface, gently gather the bottom edge of a connected petal into a fan-like shape with your fingertips. Position the connected petal directly under the center and adjust the petal ends so that they are evenly spaced and overlap slightly at their base. Tape into place (**D**). Repeat to create 7 blooms.

 3

ASSEMBLE BUDS

Trim one end of the cotton swab stick ⅓" (8 mm) from the swab. Insert the pretaped wire into the hollow of the cotton swab stem and secure it with green floral tape, covering 3" to 4" (7.5 to 10 cm) down the wire. Layer 2 squares of white tissue paper on top of each other. Place the bulb of the cotton swab in the middle of the tissue squares and wrap the swab completely. Secure the tissue tightly around the base with floral tape. Repeat for the second bud.

 4

ASSEMBLE BLOOM CLUSTER

Bend 1 bloom and 1 bud at a 60-degree angle 1½" (4 cm) from their bases. Place a second bud so its stem is flush with the bent bloom stems and attach them with floral tape 1½" (4 cm) below where the stems are bent to create a bloom cluster (**E**). Wrap and wind the tape around the 3 stems. Continue adding flowers and buds in the same manner until all are attached, adjusting spacing as necessary (**F+G**).

 5

ATTACH LEAVES

Position 2 leaves at the back of the flower about 7" (18 cm) below the base of the taped bloom stems and attach them with floral tape, wrapping 2" (5 cm) from the base of the leaves (**H**). Place 3 more leaves ½" (12 mm) below the first group of leaves, and attach the leaves to the main stem with floral tape, wrapping 2" (5 cm) down the stem. Position and attach the remaining 2 leaves to the stem at ½" (12 mm) below. Angle and position the leaves into a more natural-looking arrangement, bending them slightly at the base of each leaf (**I**). Using wire cutters, trim the main stem to 5" (13 cm) below the base of the leaves. Turn the flower upside down and wrap the cut stem end with floral tape to finish.

20
PARROT TULIP

This bold flower is pretty simple to construct and can also showcase elaborate handpainting. When I originally thought about translating its shape to paper form, I had to figure out a way to create a cupped shape without connecting the petals. The solution: moving the dart! This created a sharper angle toward the bottom of the petal so that the bell shape would stand more vertically and naturally.

GENERAL MATERIALS

- Scissors
- Green floral tape
- Fringing shears (optional)
- Two 18" (46 cm) lengths 18-gauge reinforcement wire
- Wire cutters

FOR BLOOMS

- Three 3" x 20" (7.5 x 50 cm) strips lavender tissue paper, dip-dyed fuchsia and blue (see page 16)
- Three 18" (46 cm) lengths 20-gauge pretaped wire

FOR COMPLEX STAMEN CENTER

- 2 double-headed black stamens, folded in half
- 1" x 5" (2.5 x 13 cm) strip yellow Doublette crepe paper
- 1" x 5" (2.5 x 13 cm) strip black crepe paper
- 20" (50 cm) length 18-gauge wire

FOR LEAVES

- 19" x 25" (48 x 63.5 cm) sheet green Canson paper
- Hot glue gun
- Hot glue sticks
- Three 9" (23 cm) lengths 18-gauge pretaped wire
- Three ½" x 2" (12 mm x 5 cm) pieces light-green tissue paper
- Chartreuse gouache paint
- Paintbrush

PARROT TULIP

FINISHED SIZE
Approximately 18" (46 cm)

1

PREPARE MATERIALS

Photocopy or trace the Parrot Tulip Petal template on page 169 and cut out the petal shape. Cut sixteen 3" x 3" (7.5 x 7.5 cm) pieces from the lavender tissue paper strips (16 pieces total) and stack them into 2 piles of 8 pieces each. Place the template on the stack of tissue pieces so the top of the petal is at the blue dip-dyed edge of the paper. Trace the template onto the tissue and cut it out to make a total of 16 petals.

Construct the complex stamen center using 2 double-headed black stamens following the instructions on page 23. Gather the crepe paper ¼" (6 mm) below the top of the stamen and attach it with green floral tape (**A**). Repeat with the fringed black crepe paper at the same height (**B**). Fluff.

Paint stripes across one sheet of green Canson paper with chartreuse gouache. Photocopy or trace the Parrot Tulip Leaf templates on page 166 and cut out the leaf shapes. Trace an assortment of 3 leaves onto the green Canson paper and cut them out. Assemble the leaf stems following the instructions on page 27, except glue the wire to the inside of the crease.

2

CREATE DOUBLE-PETALS

Place one petal on top of another to make a double-petal. To give the double-petals a cupped shape, add a dart (see page 25). The 3-point fold for the dart should extend from the bottom of the petals to 1" (2.5 cm) from the top (**C**). The base of the dart fold should measure about ¼" (6 mm) across and taper to a point. Gently pinch the base of each double-petal to give them a cupped shape (**D**). Repeat with the remaining petals to make a total of 8 double-petals.

3

ASSEMBLE BLOOM

Place the pinched end of one of the double-petals at the base of the Parrot Tulip center (**E**). Using as little tape as possible, attach the pinched end to the center stem with floral tape, wrapping the tape down and around the wire twice, to about ½" (12 mm) below the petal base. Place a second double-petal alongside the first, overlapping their edges by ½" (12 mm). You want to fit 4 double-petals equally spaced around the center to create your first layer. Repeat with the remaining 4 double-petals, evenly spacing them in between the other petals, overlapping the petal edges and encircling the center (**F**). Fluff the bloom slightly and bend the stem forward at a 30-degree angle about ½" (12 mm) below the base of the bloom. At this point, you will need to reinforce the stem wire, so attach one of the 18" (46 cm) reinforcement wires to the main stem by tucking the top end of the wire into the top of the gap and taping in place.

4

ASSEMBLE STEM

To shape the leaves, pull each one lengthwise across the edge of a closed pair of scissors to create a gentle curl (**G**). Place a leaf stem flush against the main bloom stem 6" (15 cm) below the main bloom. Attach to the stem with floral tape, wrapping until you reach the end of the flower stem wire (**H**). Add another reinforcement wire by laying it flush alongside the existing central stem wires and attach with floral tape. Attach the next leaf by placing it 3" (7.5 cm) below the base of the first leaf. Attach the final leaf by placing it 2" (5 cm) below the base of the previous leaf (**I**).

Using wire cutters, trim the flower stem to 4" (10 cm) below the last leaf. Turn the flower upside down and wrap the cut stem end with floral tape to finish.

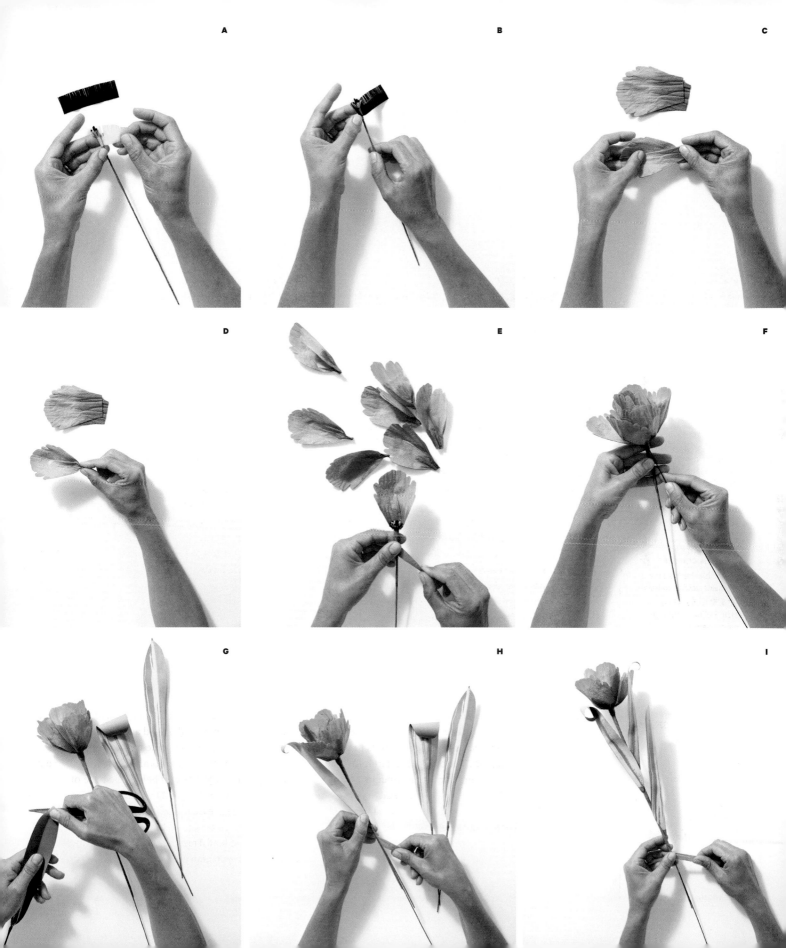

A   B   C

D   E   F

G   H   I

21
HONEYSUCKLE

Who doesn't think of summer when they smell the sweet fragrance
of the wild honeysuckle bush? Although American honeysuckle
varieties are ubiquitous in my area, I love the fan-shaped,
exotic look of the European variety best. I'm especially fascinated
by the subtle range of leaf shades, from chartreuse to pale green to
an almost evergreen hue. I discovered that handpainting a
whole sheet of Canson paper for the leaves allowed me to closely
approximate their color in nature. If you like your honeysuckle
long and abundant, like I do, you can keep adding buds and
blossoms to create a trailing vine.

GENERAL MATERIALS

- Scissors
- Green floral tape
- Wire cutters

FOR PETALS

- Three 3" x 20" (7.5 x 50 cm) strips sunset tissue paper, dip-dyed with bleach (see page 16)

FOR SIMPLE STAMEN CENTERS

- 6 double-headed yellow stamen filaments
- Six 9" (23 cm) lengths 20-gauge yellow pretaped wire

FOR BUDS

- One 3" x 20" (7.5 x 50 cm) strip sunset tissue paper, dip-dyed with bleach (see page 16)
- Four 9" (23 cm) lengths 20-gauge pretaped wire

FOR LEAVES

- 19" x 25" (48 x 63.5 cm) sheet green Canson paper
- Hot glue gun
- Hot glue sticks
- Twelve 9" (23 cm) lengths 20-gauge pretaped wire
- Twelve ½" x 2" (12 mm x 5 cm) pieces light-green tissue paper
- Dark-green gouache
- Paintbrush

HONEYSUCKLE

FINISHED SIZE
Approximately 18" (46 cm)

PREPARE MATERIALS

Photocopy or trace the Honeysuckle Petal template on page 170 and cut out the petal shape. Cut twelve 2" x 3" (5 x 7.5 cm) pieces from the tissue paper strips. Trace the petal template onto the tissue stack, positioning it so the top of the petal is at the dip-dyed edge of the paper. Cut out the petal shape to make 12 petals.

Cut eight 3" x 2" (7.5 x 5 cm) rectangles from the tissue paper strips for the buds.

Construct 6 simple stamen centers on 9" (23 cm) wires following the instructions on page 23.

Paint one sheet of green Canson paper with forest green gouache. Photocopy or trace the Honeysuckle Leaf templates on page 170 and cut out the leaf shapes. Trace 6 small leaves and 6 large leaves onto the green Canson paper and cut them out. Assemble the leaf stems following the instructions on page 27.

CONSTRUCT BLOOMS

Stack 2 petals on top of each other, and fan them out so that they overlap by ⅛" (3 mm) to create a double-petal. Run the top of your scissors over the top of the petal to create a soft curl outward (**A**). Position your simple stamen in the center of the double-petal below the curled portion, and roll the tissue around the stamen (**B**). Secure it with floral tape (**C**). Repeat with remaining 5 petal pairs and stamen centers to create a total of 6 blooms.

CONSTRUCT BUDS

Place one sunset tissue rectangle on top of another, then fold the doubled-layered rectangle in half horizontally. With the folded edge at the top, make a triangle by folding the top corners down to the center of the bottom edge (**D**). Create the shape of the bud by rolling the tissue triangle into a tube; the bud should have the right-angle point of the triangle at its top. Position a 9" (23 cm) bud wire in the bottom opening of the rolled tissue ½" (12 mm) from the bottom, then gather the base around the wire and use floral tape to securely attach the bud, taping down and around to the bottom of the wire (**E**). Finish the bud by curling the tip over the top of your fingertip to create a gentle curve. Repeat with the remaining tissue rectangles and wires to make a total of 4 buds.

ASSEMBLE BLOOM FANS

Bend 2 blooms at a 60-degree angle 1" (2.5 cm) from their bases. Place a third bloom flush against the bent bloom stems, and attach them with floral tape at the point where the stems are bent. This will create one bloom fan. Add 2 buds to the bloom fan bent at the same angle and attached at the same tape line (**F**). Wrap and wind the tape down and around the stems to about 1" (2.5 cm) below the base of the bloom fan. Repeat to make a second 3-bloom, 2-bud fan. Bend both bloom fans 1½" (4 cm) from the fan base—one at a 45-degree angle and the other at a 90-degree angle.

ASSEMBLE LEAF CLUSTER

Hold 2 of the small leaf stems with their wires flush so the leaves are positioned opposite each other and attach with floral tape. Bend one leaf at a 60-degree angle at its base. Repeat with 4 more small leaves. Add 2 large leaf stems 1" (2.5 cm) below the base of one of the small leaf clusters with their wires flush and leaves positioned opposite each other (**G**). Bend each leaf at opposing 60-degree angles and attach with floral tape. Repeat with 4 more large leaves to create a total of 3 leaf clusters. If you wish, you may vary the assortment of leaves in each cluster to create a more organic look.

ASSEMBLE STEM

Place one bloom fan stem flush to one leaf cluster wire, with the fan positioned 2" (5 cm) below the leaf cluster. Make sure to position the bloom to the left side of the leaves. Attach the bloom fan to the leaf stem with floral tape, wrapping and winding the tape to about 2" (5 cm) below the base of the bloom fan (**H**).

Attach another leaf cluster with floral tape 1" (2.5 cm) below and to the right of the bloom fan. Make sure the wires are flush and the leaves are positioned opposite each other. Bend each leaf at a 60-degree angle at its base.

Attach the second bloom fan 2" (5 cm) below the second leaf cluster and bend it at a 60-degree angle. Create a small 3-leaf set and a medium 2-leaf set. Attach the final leaf cluster 4" (10 cm) down the stem to create a balanced-looking branch. Bend each leaf at a 60-degree angle at its base.

Using wire cutters, trim the stem to 3" (7.5 cm) below the final leaf set. Turn the flower upside down and wrap the cut stem end with floral tape to finish. This plant is a delicate vine (not a straight stem), so bend the stem into a gentle S-curve to add grace and movement.

22
LILY OF THE VALLEY

Lily of the valley is a flower everyone loves. Even though the plant
is typically small and delicate, I knew its variegated
chartreuse-striped leaves would lend themselves well to a big, bold
interpretation. This supersized version utilizes the technique of
painting the Canson paper before cutting out the leaves,
for a more striking look.

GENERAL MATERIALS

- Scissors
- Green floral tape
- Wire cutters

FOR PETALS

- Two 3" x 20" (7.5 x 50 cm) strips blush tissue paper, dip-dyed with bleach (see page 16)

FOR SIMPLE STAMEN CENTER

- 5 double-headed yellow stamen filaments
- Five 12" (30.5 cm) lengths 22-gauge pretaped wire

FOR LEAVES

- 19" x 25" (48 x 63.5 cm) sheet green Canson paper
- Hot glue gun
- Hot glue sticks
- Three 9" (23 cm) lengths 18-gauge pretaped wire
- Three ½" x 2" (12 mm x 5 cm) pieces light-green tissue paper

LILY OF THE VALLEY

FINISHED SIZE
Approximately 16" (40.5 cm)

PREPARE MATERIALS

Photocopy or trace the Lily of the Valley Petal template on page 167 and cut out the petal shape. Cut the petal tissue strip into five 3" x 5" (7.5 x 13 cm) pieces and stack them. Trace the template onto the tissue and cut out the petal shape to make 5 connected petals.

Construct 5 simple stamen centers following the instructions on page 23.

Paint the sheet of green Canson paper using the gouache paint and paintbrush. Photocopy or trace the Lily of the Valley Leaf templates on page 166 and cut out the leaf shapes. Trace an assortment of 3 leaves onto the green Canson paper and cut them out. Assemble the leaf stems following the instructions on page 27.

SHAPE CONNECTED PETALS

Working on a smooth, low-friction surface, gently gather the bottom edge of a connected petal into a fanlike shape with your fingertips (**A**). Position the connected petal about 1" (2.5 cm) down one of the stems so the stamens are even with the petal ends and are visible when the flower is viewed from the side. Adjust the petal ends so that they are evenly spaced and overlap slightly at their base (**B**). Attach the connected petal with floral tape. Shape the bloom by inserting your fingertip inside the flower. Next, gently push out and smooth the gathered base of the connected petal using the round part of your index finger and your thumb (**C**). Repeat with the remaining 4 petals to create 5 blooms.

Bend each bloom at a 45-degree angle 1" (2.5 cm) below its base to the stem (**D**).

ATTACH BLOOMS

Place 2 blooms with their stems flush, positioning the angled point of the second bloom's stem 1½" (4 cm) down from the angled point of the first bloom's stem (**E**). Attach them with green floral tape, wrapping the tape down and around the wire to about 2" (5 cm) past the base of the second bloom. Add a third bloom 1½" (3.75 cm) down from the angled point of the second bloom's stem. Wrap and wind the tape down and around the wire, to about 2" (5 cm) past the base of the third bloom. Repeat to add the fourth and fifth blooms (**F**). Finish by taping 9" (23 cm) down the stem.

Create an arc in the stem by gently bending the wire in between each flower (**G**). Once you have given a pleasing line to the main stem, reposition each bloom so they all hang naturally, as if gravity were pulling them perpendicular to the ground. Take a moment to inspect the blooms—do they look natural? Adjust their spacing and angle by gently bending their stem wires if they appear too stiff or uniform.

ASSEMBLE THE STEM

To shape the leaves, pull the tip of each one lengthwise across the edge of a closed pair of scissors to create a gentle curl (**H**). Position a leaf stem 7" (18 cm) down from the base of the bloom so the tip of the leaf is the same height as the last bloom and attach it to the main stem with the floral tape (**I**). Repeat with the 2 remaining leaves, attaching them to the main stem 1" (2.5 cm) below the first leaf and on either side of the stem. Using wire cutters, trim the stem to 6" (15 cm) below the leaves. Turn the flower upside down and wrap the cut stem end with floral tape to finish.

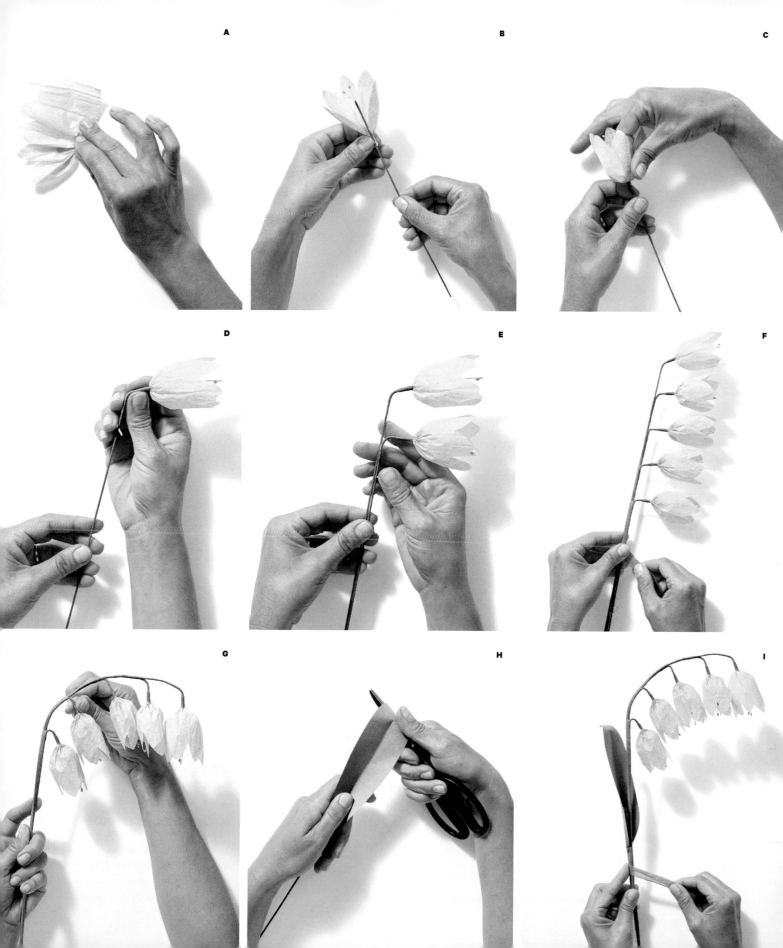

A   B   C

D   E   F

G   H   I

23

FRUIT BRANCH

My mother has an antique store, and I love the layers of patina that are created over the years on antique objects. One of my favorite objects to collect is vintage spun-cotton fruit, which I love incorporating into my paper flower pieces. You can collect your own and adapt this recipe to work with apricots, plums, pears— really any fruit that you find. Or, make your own with papier–mâché!

GENERAL MATERIALS

- Scissors
- Fringing shears (optional)
- Green floral tape
- 2 vintage cotton-spun fruits on stems (see page 173)
- 18" (46 cm) length 18-gauge reinforcement wire (optional)
- Wire cutters

FOR PETALS

- Four 3" x 20" (7.5 x 50 cm) strips peach tissue paper

FOR SIMPLE STAMEN CENTERS

- 2" x 20" (5 x 50 cm) strip sunset tissue paper
- 7 double-headed yellow stamen filaments
- Seven 9" (23 cm) lengths 20-gauge pretaped wire

FOR LEAVES

- 19" x 25" (48 x 63.5 cm) sheet lime green Canson paper
- Hot glue gun
- Hot glue sticks
- Nine 9" (23 cm) lengths pretaped 20-gauge wire
- Nine ½" x 2" (12 mm x 5 cm) pieces light-green tissue paper

FRUIT BRANCH

FINISHED SIZE
Approximately 17" (43 cm)

PREPARE MATERIALS

Photocopy or trace the Fruit Branch petal template on page 172 and cut out the petal shape. Cut thirty-six 2" x 3" (5 x 7.5 cm) pieces from the petal tissue strips. Divide them into 6 stacks of 6. Trace the petal template onto 1 stack and cut it out to make 6 petals. Repeat with the remaining stacks to make a total of 36 petals.

Construct 7 simple stamen centers on 9" (23 cm) wires following the instructions on page 23.

Photocopy or trace the Fruit Branch leaf templates on page 172 and cut out the leaf shapes. Trace 4 small and 5 large leaves onto the green Canson paper, and cut them out. Assemble the leaf stems following the instructions on page 27.

SHAPE PETALS

To give the petals a cupped shape, add a dart to each (see page 25) (**A**). The 3-point fold for the dart should extend from the bottom of the petal to ½" (12 mm) from the top. The base of the dart fold should measure about ¼" (6 mm) across and taper to a point. Repeat with the remaining petals. Gently pinch the base of each petal to give it a cupped appearance (**B**).

ASSEMBLE BLOOMS

Each fruit branch bloom is composed of 6 petals. Attach the bottom end of a petal to a center with floral tape, wrapping and winding the tape down and around the center, about 1" (2.5 cm) beyond the base (**C**). Place the next petal alongside the first, overlapping their edges by ¼" (6 mm) in a radiating fashion and encircling the center. Wrap the base with floral tape (**D**). (Note that this layer of tape and all tape for petals overlaps the layer underneath.) Repeat with 4 additional petals until the overhead view of the flower resembles a spiral. Fluff and open the bloom, adjusting the petals as needed. Repeat with the remaining petals and centers to make a total of 6 blooms, varying the amount of fluffing so that some blooms are more open than others for a more natural look.

ASSEMBLE STEM

Place one small leaf next to another with their stem wires flush, with the base of one about 1" (2.5 cm) below the base of the other. Wrap the stems together with green floral tape, wrapping from the base of the leaves to the end of the stems. Bend the lower leaf to the right at a 60-degree angle. Position one large leaf 2" (5 cm) below the small leaves on the wrapped stem. Attach the stem of the large leaf to the stem of the smaller leaves with floral tape, wrapping from the base of the large leaf to the end of the stems. Bend the large leaf to the left at a 60-degree angle. This will become your main stem.

Bend 3 blooms at 60-degree angles 1" (2.5 cm) below their bases. Place one so its wire is flush to the main stem and the blooms are 1" (2.5 cm) below the large leaf on the stem, making sure to position the bloom in front of the leaves (**E**). Using green floral tape, attach the bloom to the main stem. Repeat with two more blooms, placing them next to each other about ½" (12 mm) below the first bloom. Wrap and wind the tape down and around the stem about 2" (5 cm) below the base of the blooms.

Assemble a second leaf cluster as above with one small leaf and one large leaf (**F**). Add two fruit stems. Bend the entire stem at a 60-degree angle about 1" (2.5 cm) below the base of the fruit, place it flush against the main stem wire, and attach it with floral tape 1" (2.5 cm) below the previous 3 blooms. Create and attach another leaf cluster comprised of one small and one large leaf on the opposite side of the stem (**G**).

Bend the remaining 4 blooms at 60-degree angles, and attach them to the main stem as above, approximately 3" (7.5 cm) below the first bloom cluster (**H**).

Create one last leaf cluster comprised of two large leaves. Bend the leaf stem at a 90-degree angle 2" (5 cm) below the base of the last leaf and attach it to the main stem with floral tape 1" (2.5 cm) below the last bloom cluster (**I**). Add a reinforcement wire to fill out the stem if needed.

Using wire cutters, trim the stem to 3" (7.5 cm) below the final leaf set. Turn the branch upside down and wrap the cut end with floral tape to finish. Add a gentle bend to the branch to create a more natural, curved shape.

COLEUS

When it comes to making coleus, it's the leaves, rather than the
blooms, that shine. The stem features a simple, ruffled blue
flower with beautiful, variegated foliage you make by painting sheets
of Canson paper in different styles to produce interesting leaf
patterns. Try attaching leaf clusters in varying arrangements
to create different looks. Since the foliage is so visually interesting,
coleus makes for a gorgeous potted plant, too.

GENERAL MATERIALS

- Fringing shears (optional)
- Scissors
- Green floral tape
- Wire cutters

FOR PETALS

- Two 9" (23 cm) length 18-gauge pretaped wire
- Two 3" x 20" (7.5 x 50 cm) strips teal and purple tissue paper, hand-dyed (see page 16)

FOR LEAVES

- 9" x 25" (48 x 63.5 cm) sheet green Canson paper
- Burgundy, green, and chartreuse gouache paint
- Paintbrush
- Hot glue gun
- Hot glue sticks
- Fifteen 9" (23 cm) lengths pretaped 20-gauge wire
- Fifteen ½" x 2" (12 mm x 5 cm) pieces light-green tissue paper

COLEUS

FINISHED SIZE
Approximately 18" (46 cm)

PREPARE MATERIALS

Paint the Canson paper for the leaves. Dilute the burgundy gouache paint with enough water that it is thin enough to fall off the brush easily. Load a medium brush with the paint and tap the handle as you move the brush across the sheet of paper to create a splatter pattern. Let the sheet dry flat. Repeat with the green and then chartreuse paint, allowing ample time for the paint to dry in between applications.

Photocopy or trace the Coleus Leaf templates on page 167 and cut out the leaf shapes. Trace 6 small, 6 medium, and 3 large leaves onto the green Canson paper, and cut them out. Assemble the leaf stems following the instructions on page 27.

CREATE BLOOMS

Holding it vertically with the folded edge to the right, trim the strip on the diagonal, so that the top portion measures 1" (2.5 cm) and gradually gets thicker until you reach the full width of the strip at the bottom. Fold one 3" x 20" (7.5 x 50 cm) strip in half lengthwise. Cut a ⅓" (8 mm) fringe on the folded edge. Repeat with the second stripe.

Beginning with the thinner end, wrap the tissue around and down the stem to create a 2" (5 cm) spiraled fringe (**A**). Press the tissue to the floral tape underneath. Using green floral tape, secure the fringed tissue to the center stem wire. Continue to wrap the stem with floral tape until you reach 3" (7.5 cm) below the fringe (**B**). Repeat to create the second bloom.

ASSEMBLE STEM

Position 3 small leaf stems flush to the first Coleus stem, about 2" (5 cm) down the stem from the center, so that the leaves completely encircle the center. Before attaching to the stem of the flower, bend all leaves at a 30-degree angle ½" (12 mm) down the stem from the base of the leaf. Attach the leaves with floral tape, wrapping the stems 2" (5 cm) below the base of the leaves (**C**). Attach 3 medium leaves in a cluster like the first three 2" (5 cm) below the first, and then repeat with the 3 large leaves, taping 2" (5 cm) down the stem as you attach each cluster (**D**). Attach 3 small leaves 2" (5 cm) down the second Coleus stem as above. Then add 3 medium leaves 2" (5 cm) below that. Bend the second stem at a 90-degree angle about 2" (5 cm) below the last leaf cluster (**E**). Lay it flush to the main stem about 3" (7.5 cm) down, and attach with floral tape (**F**). Using wire cutters, trim the stem to 4" (10 cm) below the final leaf set. Adjust and angle the leaves. Turn the flower upside down and wrap the cut stem end with floral tape to finish.

A

B

C

D

F

E

25

DELPHINIUM

If you remember the towering hollyhock from my first book, you'll find this project just as enjoyable to create. The tall stem works beautifully as a single stem or as part of a larger arrangement. The blooms of varied size and color are lots of fun to play around with—I like to make them in purple and blue or peach and white tissue, but you can try them in any color combination you like. Just like hollyhocks, delphiniums require reinforcement wire to support their height.

GENERAL MATERIALS

- Scissors
- Green floral tape
- Four 18" (46 cm) lengths 18-gauge reinforcement wire
- Wire cutters

FOR PETALS

- Twenty-two 3" x 20" (7.5 x 50 cm) strips white tissue paper dip-dyed with blue dye (see page 16)

FOR SMALL POM-POM CENTERs

- 20" x 60" (50 x 152 cm) sheet black fine crepe paper
- Twenty-five 9" (23 cm) lengths 20-gauge pretaped wire

FOR LEAVES

- 19" x 25" (48 x 63.5 cm) sheet lime green Canson paper
- Hot glue gun
- Hot glue sticks
- Three 9" (23 cm) lengths 18-gauge pretaped wire
- Three ½" x 2" (12 mm x 5 cm) pieces light-green tissue paper

DELPHINIUM

FINISHED SIZE
Approximately 30" (76 cm)

1

PREPARE MATERIALS

Photocopy or trace the Small and Large Delphinium Petal templates on page 170 and cut out the connected petal shapes. Cut twenty-five 3" x 6" (7.5 x 15 cm) pieces from the tissue strips and set the rest aside. Divide the pieces into 5 stacks of 5 pieces each. Place the small petal template on 1 stack, with the top of the petal at the painted edge of the paper. Trace the template onto the tissue and cut it out to make 5 petals. Repeat with the remaining stacks to make 25 petals total. Using the remaining tissue strips, cut twenty-seven 3" x 8" (7.5 x 20 cm) pieces. Divide the pieces into 3 stacks of 9 pieces each. Place the large petal template on 1 stack, with the top of the petal at the painted edge of the paper. Trace the template onto the tissue and cut it out to make 9 petals. Repeat with the remaining stacks to make 27 petals total.

Construct 25 small pom-pom centers following the instructions on page 22, substituting black fine crepe paper for the yellow tissue.

Photocopy or trace the Delphinium Leaf template on page 170 and cut out the shape. Trace 3 leaves onto the green Canson paper and cut them out. Assemble the leaf stems following the instructions on page 27.

2

ASSEMBLE BLOOMS

The Delphinium stem shown here is comprised of 25 total blooms—12 small (with 1 small connected petal), 6 medium (with 1 small and 1 large connected petal), and 7 large (with 1 small and 3 large connected petals).

Working on a smooth, low-friction surface, gently gather the bottom edge of one small connected petal into a fanlike shape with your fingertips (**A**). Press the gathered edge of the petal to encircle the entire pom-pom stamen center, making sure the petal stays gathered (**B**). Attach with floral tape. Wrap the tape down and around the wire to about 1" (2.5 cm) below the base of the floret. Repeat with the remaining 24 small connected petals and 24 pom-pom stamen centers to

create 24 more blooms. Set 12 aside—these will be your small blooms.

To create the medium blooms, gather 6 existing small bloom stems and 6 large connected petals. Working on a smooth, low-friction surface, gently gather the bottom edge of one large connected petal into a fanlike shape with your fingertips. Press the gathered edge of the petal to encircle one of the small blooms, making sure the petal stays gathered. Attach with floral tape. Wrap the tape down and around the wire to about 1" (2.5 cm) below the base of the floret. Repeat with 5 large connected petals and 5 small bloom stems to create 6 medium blooms.

To create the large blooms, gather the remaining 7 existing small bloom stems and the remaining 21 large connected petals. Working on a smooth, low-friction surface, gently gather the bottom edge of one large connected petal into a fanlike shape with your fingertips. Press the gathered edge of the petal to encircle one of the small blooms, making sure the petal stays gathered. Attach with floral tape. Wrap the tape down and around the wire to about 1" (2.5 cm) below the base of the floret. Repeat with 2 more large petals to create 1 large bloom. Repeat the whole process with the remaining 18 large connected petals and the remaining 6 small bloom stems to create 7 large blooms.

3

BEGIN ASSEMBLING STEM

The delphinium will be constructed with the smallest blooms at the top of the wire and the largest blooms and leaves at the bottom. To begin, select 2 small blooms and bend 1 slightly 1" (2.5 cm) below the base of the bloom, so they do not touch (and crush) each other as you work. Attach the bent bloom to the straight bloom 1" (2.5 cm) below the bloom base, wrapping 1" (2.5 cm) down the stems—this will become your main stem (**C**). Bend, position, and attach 3 more small blooms 1" (2.5 cm) below the base of the first grouping, creating a second tier (**D**). Bend, position, and attach 3 more small blooms 1" (2.5 cm) below the base of the second-tier blooms, creating a third tier. Bend, position, and attach 3 more small blooms 1" (2.5 cm) below the base of the third-tier blooms, creating a fourth tier.

At this point, add a reinforcement wire. Tuck the top end of the reinforcement wire into the gap that was created when the existing wires were taped together. Attach the reinforcement wire to the main stem by wrapping it with floral tape 6" (15 cm) down the flower stem.

Bend 3 medium blooms and position them 1" (2.5 cm) below the base of the previous tier (**E**). Attach the blooms, wrapping 2" (5 cm) down the main stem, creating a fifth tier of blooms, and then repeat with the 3 remaining medium blooms to create a sixth tier.

Bend 2 large blooms and position them below the base of the previous tier so that the flowers barely touch each other. Attach the blooms, wrapping 2" (5 cm) down the main stem, creating a seventh tier of blooms (**F**).

At this point, add another reinforcement wire. Bend, position, and attach 2 more large blooms below the base of the seventh-tier blooms, creating an eighth tier. Bend, position, and attach the 3 remaining large blooms to create a ninth and final tier. Readjust blooms so that they all have pleasing spacing. The blooms should just barely touch. If you need to add further reinforcement, do so now with the 2 remaining wires.

FINISH ASSEMBLING STEM
Attach the leaves to frame the bottom tier of flowers. Bend each leaf forward at a 60-degree angle at its base. Place a leaf stem flush to the main stem, positioning the leaf just below the unfurling bloom, and attach it with floral tape (**G**). Wrap the tape down the full length of the stem. Attach the second leaf stem opposite the first, positioning it on the opposite side of the stem (**H**). Attach the third leaf stem, positioning it between the other 2. Using wire cutters, trim the flower stem so it extends 7" (18 cm) beyond the last leaf. Turn the flower upside down and wrap the cut stem end with floral tape to finish.

26

LUPINE

When I look at the masses of lupine that crop up along the
highway with no apparent water source, I'm blown away by their
ability to survive. They are hardy yet delicate—a wonderful
blend of form and function whose leaves are designed in
such a way as to perfectly catch water and funnel it to the center.
Constructing one from paper is as easy as it is gorgeous.

GENERAL MATERIALS

- Scissors
- Green floral tape
- Two 18" (46 cm) lengths 18-gauge reinforcement wire
- Wire cutters

FOR PETALS

- Five 3" x 20" (7.5 x 50 cm) strips plum tissue paper, dip-dyed with water (see page 16)
- Five 3" x 20" (7.5 x 50 cm) strips white tissue paper, dip-dyed with water (see page 16)
- Twenty-two 9" (23 cm) lengths 20-gauge pretaped wire

FOR BUDS

- 3" x 20" (7.5 x 50 cm) strip plum tissue paper, dip-dyed with water (see page 16)
- Five 6" (15 cm) lengths 20-gauge pretaped wire

FOR LEAVES

- 19" x 25" (48 x 63.5 cm) sheet green Canson paper
- Hot glue gun
- Hot glue sticks
- Three 9" (23 cm) lengths 18-gauge pretaped wire
- Three ½" x 2" (12 mm x 5 cm) pieces light-green tissue paper

LUPINE

FINISHED SIZE
Approximately 18" (46 cm)

PREPARE MATERIALS

Photocopy or trace the Lupine Petal template on page 163 and cut out the petal shape. Cut thirty 3" x 3" (7.5 x 7.5 cm) pieces from the plum and 30 pieces from the white tissue paper strips, and divide each into 6 stacks of 5. Place the template on 1 stack of tissue pieces so the top of the petal is at the dip-dyed edge of the paper. Trace the template onto the tissue and cut it out. Repeat with the remaining stacks to make 60 petals—30 petals in each color.

For the buds, cut ten 2" x 2" (5 x 5 cm) squares from the 3" x 20" (7.5 x 50 cm) strip of plum tissue paper.

Photocopy or trace the Lupine Leaf template on page 163 and cut out the leaf shape. Trace 3 leaves onto the green Canson paper and cut them out. Assemble the leaf stems following the instructions on page 27.

CREATE BLOOMS

Place one plum petal on top of one white petal to create a double-petal (**A**). Fold the double-petal in half to make a 4-layered petal (**B**). Gently gather the base of the petal. Holding the gathered end, bring the outside edges together, as if folding in half once more, to create a rounded shape (**C**). Attach the gathered end of the petal to a 9" (23 cm) wire with green floral tape. Wrap the tape down and around the wire to 2" (5 cm) below the base of the bloom (**D+E**). Repeat with the remaining petals and wires to make a total of 22 blooms. Lay the blooms out in a line, and carefully separate the layers of tissue to open each bloom. Start by fluffing the first bloom a little bit, the second a bit more, and so on, until the blooms show a progression, from slightly open to completely unfurled.

ASSEMBLE BUDS

Place one plum tissue square on top of another, then fold the doubled-layered square in half horizontally. With the folded edge at the top, make a triangle by folding the top corners down to the center of the bottom edge (**F**). Create the shape of the bud by rolling the tissue triangle into a tube; the bud should have the right-angle point of the triangle at its top. Position a 4" (10 cm) bud wire ¼" (6 mm) from the bottom of the rolled tissue, then gather the base around the wire and tape securely down to the bottom of the wire (**G+H**). Repeat with the remaining tissue squares and wires to make a total of 5 buds.

ASSEMBLE STEM

The lupine stem is assembled with the buds at the top, progressing down to the smallest blooms, with the most unfurled blooms placed at the very bottom. To begin assembling, bend 2 buds at a 60-degree angle 1" (2.5 cm) from their bases and attach them to a third bud at the point where the stems are bent to create a 3-bud cluster (**I**). Wrap the tape down and around the stems about 1" (2.5 cm) below the base. Bend the remaining 2 buds at a 60-degree angle, and attach them 1" (2.5 cm) farther down the stem. Next, bend 3 blooms at a 60-degree angle 1" (5 cm) from their bases and attach them to the stem one at a time (**J**). Adjust them in a pleasing manner around the buds, about 1" (2.5 cm) apart in even rows. Repeat the process, adding bunches of 4 to 5 blooms, until you have filled in the stem with the remaining blooms. To create the stem shown here, I used 1 row of 3 blooms, followed by a row of 4 and 3 rows of 5 (**K**).

ATTACH LEAVES

Bend the 3 leaf stems at a 60-degree angle 3" (7.5 cm) from their base and attach them to the stem, positioning them 2" (5 cm) below the last row of blooms (**L**). Attach two reinforcement wires to fill out the base of the stem. Place each reinforcement wire alongside the main stem and insert the top end of the wire into the base of the bloom. Holding them flush to the main stem, attach the reinforcement wires to the stem by wrapping them with floral tape the full length of the flower stem.

Using wire cutters, trim the stem to 7" (18 cm) below the last row of leaves. Turn the flower upside down and finish the cut stem with floral tape. Pull the stem into a gentle curl and then reposition the blooms (**M**).

PART 2

THE PROJECTS

NOW THAT YOU'VE HAD A CHANCE TO CREATE THE basic stems and see how they are constructed, it's time to play around with size, shape, color, and quantity to create extraordinary projects. This is where you think about various ways to arrange the blooms, buds, leaves, and stems together—along with other ingredients—to put the geometry of design into play. In other words, it's your chance to see how these bigger ideas can come together in unexpected ways by combining and modifying the single stem shapes.

These projects are all geared toward entertaining or adding some flair to your home. I think of them in three categories—Single-Stem Elaborations, Festive Décor, and Bold Arrangements. They work by putting together the single stems in new and interesting combinations by working with groupings of shapes and textures—spikes shine in the Delphinium Centerpiece on page 159, saucers make up the Oversize Nashi Blossom on page 156, and rectangles are the focus in the Bearded Iris Wreath on page 154. Other projects focus on a single geometric theme, like the cones in play in the Blooming Chandelier on page 154. Flip through the gallery of projects on the following pages to see what speaks to you. Then, turn to each design's page for instructions for how to put them together. No matter which project you choose to make, the blooms will add up to extraordinary!

PEONY
BOUQUET
PG 161

VICTORIAN
ARRANGEMENT
PG 160

GARDEN
ROSE PETAL
VARIATIONS
PG 152

138

DELPHINIUM
CENTERPIECE
PG 159

BLOOMING
CHANDELIER
PG 154

OVERSIZE
NASHI
BLOSSOM
PG 156

COLEUS
PLANT LEAVES
PG 150

RHODODENDRON
WALL HANGING
PG 155

MINI
ARRANGEMENT
PG 159

WILD ROSE
GARLAND
PG 158

ALLIUM
VARIATIONS
PG 152

CREATING
BULBS
PG 151

BEARDED
IRIS WREATH
PG 154

DUTCH STILL-LIFE
CENTERPIECE
PG 161

MARIGOLD
CURTAIN
GARLAND
PG 153

SINGLE-STEM ELABORATIONS

Coleus
Plant Leaves
PAGE 141

I am inspired by all of the incredibly different, striking leaf patterns expressed by the many varieties of the coleus plant. In paper, the effect is easy to re-create with gouache paint and simple brushstrokes. If you love mixing and matching patterns as much as I do, this project is a wonderful opportunity to play with technique and color to create a beautiful overall effect.

PREPARE MATERIALS
You will need pink, burgundy, green, and rust Canson paper; pink, burgundy, lime green, white, yellow, green, red, and rust gouache paint; a soft, natural-bristled paintbrush; and scissors. Follow the instructions on page 17 to make leaves painted several ways—striped, splattered, solid then splattered, solid then edged in color, and more—using the Coleus Leaf templates on page 167 as a base. Once you have created the leaves, use the instructions and supplies on page 27 to make 3 coleus stems.

ARRANGE STEMS
This project is a fun way to experiment with technique and color. When you're ready to display the final creation, cut the stems to different heights and arrange them in a medium-size vessel. Then, take a minute to position the piece—move the leaves into open spaces, and position each element to "catch the sunlight."

Creating Bulbs
PAGE 146

There is something unique about seeing the entire bulb on a single stem of a flower. I was inspired to create this project when I was bleaching some plain brown and tan tissue for another project and it turned unexpectedly wonderful colors—the browns bleached to purple then green, becoming the perfect papers for creating a bulb.

PREPARE MATERIALS

You will need scissors; one 6" x 20" (15 x 50 cm) strip tan tissue paper, dip-dyed in bleach (see page 16) with a 3" (7.5 cm) fringe cut on the blue side; one 6" x 20" (15 x 50 cm) strip brown tissue paper, dip-dyed in bleach (see page 16) with a 3" (7.5 cm) fringe cut on the brown side; green floral tape; 1 Narcissus (page 96), Parrot Tulip (page 104), or Easter Lily (page 92); and four 4" x 20" (10 x 50 cm) strips brown tissue paper.

CREATE BULB

First crinkle the tan tissue in your hand multiple times to break it down and create a crinkly look. Unfurl the paper and, working on a smooth, low-friction surface, gently gather the unfringed side together into a fanlike shape with your fingertips, keeping the paper's edges parallel (**A**). The fringed side becomes the "roots." Then, using the floral tape, attach it to the bottom of the flower stem (**B**). Take 3 of the 4 plain brown strips and gather them up in your palm to make 3 balls (just like a bud ball; see page 24). Fold the brown strip in half so you have a doubled 10" (25 cm) strip. Fold the top half over by 1½" (4 cm) and arrange the 3 balls under the folded flap (**C**).

Position the stem so that the roots extend over the folded edge of the flap. Roll the strip lengthwise (with crinkled balls inside) around the stem to create a padded ball with the roots sticking out the bottom (**D**). Tape the remaining tissue in place to the top of the stem. Crinkle the remaining dip-dyed brown fringed strip in your hands, unfurl, and then wrap around the bulb. Twist the roots together and tape the top paper in place with the floral tape (**F**). Once you get the hang of this, you can customize the bulb to fit larger or smaller stems. I like to stake these into potted plants, just like you'd see with a potted plant during the holidays.

Garden Rose Petal Variations
PAGE 137

I was so pleased when the owner of Astier de Villatte, an amazing shop in Paris, asked me to make a Charles de Gaulle rose—his favorite rose variety—for their opening. I tried many combinations of petal shapes and center constructions, but finally, I found that if I varied the center a bit and made a slight tweak to the petal, I could capture the look of this gorgeous flower. In playing around with the flower, I realized that there was almost an endless number of stunning variations, each involving just a slight change to the basic rose center and petal shape. Together, these slight tweaks make a beautiful visual feast that I think you'll love as much as I do.

PREPARE MATERIALS

You will need scissors; tissue paper in shades of purple, pink, and blue; and materials for dyeing and painting petals. You will also need green floral tape and wire cutters. Follow the instructions on pages 16–17 to make an assortment of dyed, painted, and bleached petals using the Eden Rose Petal templates on page 169 as a base. You can see my examples on pages 2 and 137.

CREATE BLOOMS

Once you have created the petals, follow the instructions and supplies on page 40 for making an assortment of Eden Roses. I invite you to take the opportunity to experiment, take what you have learned, and run with it, the way I did during my experience making flowers for Astier de Villatte. Use more or fewer petals to create variations—larger petals for an oversize bloom or just the small petals for a delicate bud. You can also experiment with mixing petal colors, even in one bloom. I like to include petals that range from light to dark purples, and even some blues. Use this project as a chance to see what you like and play around with form and function to create your own unique take on the flower.

Allium Variations
PAGE 145

This is an arrangement that shows the diversity of the flower. When I was a child, we grew garlic. We let some of the plants go to seed—then they blossomed into beautiful globe-shaped flowers, so this project is one that brings back fond childhood memories. I'm also inspired by ornamental alliums that come in a variety of sizes, shapes, and density of blooms. In any arrangement, the allium's globe shape is a wonderful accent. Here, the globes are gorgeous all massed together!

VARYING FORM

Make as many allium blossoms (page 30) as you'll want for the arrangement. I made 6. Once you decide how many, consider how you might vary their size and color. Use your imagination—add additional flowers, add fewer blooms, create a smaller globe by shortening the stems of the individual florets, or lengthen them to make the bloom larger. As you can see by referring back to the photo on page 145, any way you mix and match will result in a beautiful piece.

FESTIVE DÉCOR

**Marigold Curtain
Garland**
PAGE 149

If you've ever hoped for endless strings of flowers to adorn your home, this is your chance to live the dream. Inspired by the abundant use of marigolds at Indian weddings, this curtain of blooms is a super-fun project that is impactful and visually stunning. Here, I used simple Fluffy Poppy blossoms (which are dead ringers for marigolds) in a variety of colors, punctuated by pops of Lily of the Valley. Once you string them together, you'll never want to take this garland down.

PREPARE MATERIALS

You will need one hundred eighty 3" x 20" (7.5 x 50 cm) orange tissue strips; thirty 3" x 20" (7.5 x 50 cm) purple tissue strips; thirty 3" x 20" (7.5 x 50 cm) hot pink tissue strips; and one 5" (13 cm) purple tissue strip.

Make 180 Fluffy Poppy blossoms (page 42) using the orange tissue strips, taping the petals together without using wire. Then, create 30 Fluffy Poppies from the purple strips, 30 Fluffy Poppies from the hot pink tissue strips, and one large Poppy from the 5" (13 cm) purple strip. You will also need to create 20 large bells by blowing up the Lily of the Valley Petal template on page 168 by 200 percent, using two 4" x 7" (10 x 18 cm) sheets aqua tissue instead of 1 for each bloom to make them stronger, omitting the wire. Follow the instructions and supplies on page 114, omitting the stamen and wire, and tape the ends of tissue together. You will also need an upholstery needle; a roll of Japanese paper twine; one 36" (91 cm) bamboo rod; scissors; and green floral tape.

ASSEMBLE GARLAND

With the upholstery needle threaded with twine, poke a hole straight up through the middle of an orange Fluffy Poppy. Repeat to attach the remaining orange blooms; create 6 garlands of 30 orange blooms each, leaving a few feet of twine at the bottom of each garland. Tie each to the bamboo rod with a double knot to hang them. Once all of the garlands are attached, gather them together and loosely tie remaining twine tails together and trim.

Repeat the process to create 6 more garlands using 5 purple and hot pink blooms each, alternating the colors. Leave a few feet of twine at the bottom of each garland. Tie the top of the purple and pink garlands together, and attach the cluster to the bottom of the orange garland cluster using a double knot. Thread the upholstery needle one more time, and use it to string the 20 aqua bells on at random heights. Attach 1 large Fluffy Poppy to cover the space where the first two garlands meet. Trim away the remaining thread, as needed.

Blooming Chandelier
PAGE 139

One of the most stylistically influential people in my life is florist Kelly Kornegay, for whom I worked at Rayon Vert in San Francisco. She has beautiful taste in clothing, décor, and flowers, and we share a love of Easter lilies, which she insists on calling "Longiflorum" (from *Lilium longiflorum*, their Latin name). The style of this project is inspired by her aesthetic. Although I've used Easter Lilies here, this is a great way to display any of your blooms. Just hang them from the ceiling like beautiful freeform objects. Or adorn an existing chandelier to turn your dining room into a great party space!

PREPARE MATERIALS

This chandelier is approximately 32" tall x 26" wide (81 x 66 cm). For this project, you will need 4 single Easter Lily stems, 1 double Easter Lily stem, 1 double Easter Lily stem with a single bud, 1 single Easter Lily stem with a single bud, and 6 Cornflowers (pages 94 and 54) in assorted colors. For all Lily stems, add half the leaves specified to each stem, and then reserve the rest to use in assembly. You will also need green floral tape, five to six 18" (46 cm) lengths 16-gauge reinforcement wire, wire cutters, a 18" x 12" (46 x 30.5 cm) paper lantern (optional), and a length of ribbon and a ceiling hook, for hanging.

ASSEMBLE THE CHANDELIER

Before you start taping flowers together, map out where you'd like each bloom to go, keeping in mind that this is a three-dimensional object, not a flat piece. I like to add a bit of space between each bloom to allow the eye to rest. To begin, tape any 2 Lilies together, then add in a stem of Cornflower to soften the bolder Lily form. Continue by adding another Lily, and then a reinforcement wire. Continue adding flowers down the stem, alternating between Lilies and Cornflowers, and adding in the extra leaves (the ones you reserved) in regular intervals to the main stem as you go. Once you reach the end, curve the bottom of the stem up to create a hook from which you can hang a small paper lantern, if you wish.

HANG THE CHANDELIER

I had a preexisting chandelier, so I used a chandelier cap and chain to hang mine. However, you can simply cut a piece of beautiful ribbon and suspend yours from a hook in the ceiling.

Bearded Iris Wreath
PAGE 147

This is my take on a Roman myrtle wreath—open at the top and attached in the middle at its base. Because the Bearded Iris blossom is a rectangular flower, I played off its shape with an open rectangular wreath as a variation on the traditional circular wreath shape—you can just rest it on the mantel instead of hanging it, if you wish. I use more leaves here than in the single stem project to highlight the rectangular and linear aspects.

PREPARE MATERIALS

This wreath is approximately 36" tall x 28" wide (91 x 71 cm). You will need 16 Bearded Iris blooms, approximately 45 Bearded Iris leaves, and 11 Bearded Iris buds (page 80). You will also need 1" (2.5 cm) green floral tape, approximately twenty-five 18" (46 cm) lengths 16-gauge reinforcement wire, wire cutters, and one 36" (91 cm) silk ribbon.

PREPARE STEMS

When working on a larger project, I like to create all the blooms first, then all the buds, and finally I attach them together to create small clusters. Think about clustering blooms of the same colors together and mixing in some variegated or handpainted leaves to break up the solid colors. For example, make a few stems that contain 1 bloom and 1 leaf. Then, create a few larger clusters, like a bloom with a bud and a few leaves. Once you create all the clusters, lay everything out on a tabletop or the ground so you can view them together all at once.

ASSEMBLE WREATH

The wreath is composed of 2 separate Bearded Iris garlands that are taped together in the middle. To begin, select 2 nice clusters and tape them together to create the top of one side. I like to use 1" (2.5 cm) wide floral tape because it makes the larger, more cumbersome pieces easier to tape. Work your way down, continuing to add stem clusters and reinforcement wires as needed. Fill in the empty spaces with leaves as you go. Once you have created a 36" (91 cm) segment, bend the wire at a 90-degree angle and continue adding a few more leaves, blooms, and buds to make a 14" (35.5 cm) "L" shape. Repeat to create the other half of the wreath, this time bending the 90-degree angle the opposite way to make a backward "L" (I made the right side slightly taller than the left, for a more natural effect). Using wire cutters, trim the extra stems on the bottom of the "L" to 3" (7.5 cm) and tape the two sides together at this point. Then wrap the silk ribbon over the taped connection to hide it and tie in a bow.

**Rhododendron
Wall Hanging**
PAGE 142

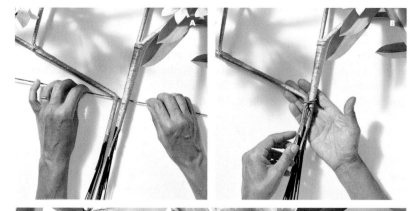

This hanging is inspired by the seventies artist Curtis Jeré, known for making sculptural wall art from bronze—statement pieces for sure! My paper interpretation can be made as large or as small as you like. I recommend customizing it to the wall that you want to hang it on.

(1)

PREPARE MATERIALS

This hanging is approximately 5' x 4½' (1.5 x 1.4 m). For this project, you will need 10 Rhododendron bloom clusters (page 52) with 10 to 12 blooms in each cluster. You will also need to make leaf clusters from 75 Rhododendron leaves in assorted sizes. To create them, begin by painting 3 sheets of apple green Canson paper with gold paint and make leaf stems following the instructions and supplies on page 27. Tape the leaf stems together to create 5 large clusters of 9 leaves each, and 5 smaller clusters of 6 smaller leaves each. You will also need approximately twenty-five 18" (46 cm) lengths 16-gauge reinforcement wire, green floral tape, gold floral tape, and a frame anchor for hanging (optional).

(2)

ASSEMBLE THE BRANCHES

Attach the bloom clusters to the leaf clusters to make 4 smaller branches. Add reinforcement wires as you go, as needed. You will initially attach the stems with green floral tape, then add a final layer of gold floral tape to create the bronze effect. Once you have the branches ready, lay them out on a flat surface to decide on your design before you attach them to each other. There should be some dense areas of blooms, some lighter areas, and some areas where you see the branch itself. Then, begin to tape the branches together to create the main branch. These branches will become quite heavy, so for extra strength, attach each branch to the other using a pretaped reinforcement wire as a tie and completely wrap with gold floral tape to tighten the bond (**A–C**).

If you want to hang your project once it is completed, create two wire loops by taping two reinforcement wires with gold floral tape and bending them into a loop shape (as in the Wild Rose Garland project on page 158). Tape the loops on the main center branch halfway down the stem with gold floral tape. This project is on the heavier side, so I recommend hanging it permanently on your wall as you would hang a painting with a frame anchor.

This Oversize Nashi Blossom is based on the window display I was commissioned to create for Jo Malone—a London-based perfume and skincare company—inspired by one of their signature colognes, which has notes of this Japanese springtime bloom. These oversize blossoms are perfect for creating abundant party décor. Or, simply hang one large bloom on your wall as a unique art piece.

GATHER MATERIALS

This blossom is approximately 28" (71 cm) wide. For this project, you will need scissors, white tissue paper dip-dyed (see page 16) pink, peach, or lime green (for blossoms), yellow tissue paper dip-dyed lime green (for blossom center), a hot glue gun and hot glue sticks, 14 white and 7 yellow 18" (46 cm) lengths pretaped 16-gauge wire, polymer clay (such as FIMO), and 1" (2.5 cm) wide yellow, light green, and white floral tape.

PREPARE MATERIALS

Photocopy or trace the Nashi Petal template on page 164 and cut out the petal shape. Cut fourteen 15" x 20" (38 x 50 cm) pieces of the white dip-dyed tissue paper for the blossom. Place the template on the stack of tissue pieces and cut it out to make 14 petals. Then, cut three 7" x 20" (18 x 50 cm) lime green tissue paper strips.

CREATE DOUBLE-PETALS

Place a petal on a flat surface and use a hot glue gun to glue 2 of the white 18" (46 cm) 16-gauge wires ½" (4 cm) from the bottom edge of the petal. Glue another petal on top of the first, edges aligned, so that the 2 petals sandwich the wire (**A**). Repeat with remaining petals, glue, and wire to create a total of 7 double-petals.

CREATE CENTER

Since this plant is oversized, you will have to create your own stamens. I like to use FIMO polymer clay for this purpose. Start with a marble-sized piece of clay, and mold it into the shape of an olive. Use 1 of the yellow 18" (46 cm) 16-gauge wires to poke a hole halfway up through the center on the long side where the wire will be inserted after the clay is baked and then put the wire aside. Repeat to create 6 more stamens. Bake solid following the instructions on the clay package. Remove and let cool. Fill the hole with a bit of hot glue and insert the wire (**B**).

Using scissors, make a 3½" (9 cm) fringe along one side of the 3 lime green tissue paper strips.

Gather the stamens in your hand so that they are even with each other. Using the green floral tape, secure them 7" (18 cm) below the clay base. Next, arrange the stamens in a radiating spray. Working on a smooth, low-friction surface, gently gather up the unfringed edge of one lime green tissue paper strip into a fanlike shape with your fingertips (**C**). Press the pinched end in place, covering a third of the space at the base of the stamens. Secure with 1" (2.5 cm) green floral tape. Repeat with the remaining strips (**D**).

CREATE BLOOMS

Pinch the end of 1 petal into a fan shape and hold the pinched end to the center so that it covers half of the space around the center (**E+F**). Wrap floral tape down and around the wires to about 1" (2.5 cm) beyond the base. Place the second petal where the first petal ends, overlapping the edges by ½" (12 mm) and encircling the other half of the center. Wrap the base with green floral tape. Repeat with the remaining petals, staggering them below the first 2 petals, filling in any gaps. Using wire cutters, trim the stem to your desired length. Turn the flower upside down and wrap the cut stem end with floral tape to finish.

A

B

C

This is a fun way create a big impact for your next fete, using inexpensive premade party décor—paper garlands, honeycomb fans, and honeycomb balls—accented with handmade blooms. I like the idea of loosely throwing the garlands together for a more modern approach!

① PREPARE MATERIALS

This garland is approximately 6' (1.8 m) long. For this project, you will need 5 Desert Rose stems (page 64) with the Canson paper for the leaves painted forest green. You will also need approximately 10 store-bought garlands, 8 honeycomb fans, and 2 honeycomb balls to fill in the space, as well as pretaped floral wire, floral tape, wire cutters, and temporary hooks and thin cotton twine to attach the décor to your wall.

② ASSEMBLE GARLAND

Add a loop made of pretaped floral wire to the back of first bloom and a hook made of the pretaped wire at the back of the last bloom (**A–C**). Once the flower segments are created, they can be taped together to create the garland as desired. To attach this project temporarily to the wall for a special event, you can use disposable hooks (I like 3M). Then, tie a loop of decorative twine to the top loops of the garlands and tissue paper elements and hang as needed from the hooks.

BOLD ARRANGEMENTS

Mini Arrangement
PAGE 143

Creating small bouquets as favors or thank-yous is a great way to present your creations without making a full-scale arrangement. This mini arrangement is the perfect hostess gift, but it can also be a charming final touch to a gorgeous package.

PREPARE MATERIALS

For this project you will need 1 Lilac, (see Peegee Hydrangea on page 74), 1 Fern frond template (page 162), assembled as shown on page 27 with red Canson paper, 2 Rhododendron (page 52), Desert Rose (page 64), or Coleus leaves (page 17), and 2 Fluffy Poppies created with 2" x 20" (5 x 31 cm) tissue paper strips (page 44). You will also need green floral tape, wire cutters, and ½" (12 mm) silk ribbon or washi decorative tape.

CREATE BOUQUET

Position the stems together in a pleasing manner. Bend them slightly here and there to create a natural look. The Lilac is the star—place it in the middle front. Use the Fern positioned in the back, to frame the Lilac. Finish with the Fluffy Poppies low and in the front, so that they cover the mechanics and stems. Secure with floral tape and trim stems to your desired length with wire cutters. Turn the arrangement upside down and wrap the cut stem end with floral tape to finish.

PREPARE PACKAGE

To attach a small bouquet to a package, simply wrap the gift and place the small bouquet on top. Either tie it directly to the package with silk ribbon used to wrap the gift, or secure it with washi decorative tape.

Delphinium Centerpiece
PAGE 138

This arrangement is a good project for experimenting with floral geometry because it's so dynamic, playing the spike shape of the Delphiniums off of the globe shape of Alliums. And I just love massive groupings of Delphiniums because the variety of size and shape only adds to the visual impact of the project. With a simple tweak of the template, you can make the Allium blossoms in greatly varied sizes and shapes.

PREPARE MATERIALS

This arrangement is approximately 36" x 36" (91 x 91 cm) when completed. To start, make 8 assorted Delphiniums (page 126), 5 assorted Alliums (page 32) with 5 Allium leaves painted a dark blue-green (see page 17), 5 Lilies of the Valley (page 114), 7 Hellebores (page 68), and two Fern fronds (page 162, assembled as shown on page 27). You will also need scissors, Styrofoam sheet, 1 large bowl, floral sticky clay (optional), and wire cutters.

PREPARE BOWL

Cut a piece of Styrofoam to fit tightly in the bowl, making sure it falls about 1" (2.5 cm) below the lip of the bowl. If the Styrofoam is not tightly wedged in, secure it with a small piece or two of floral sticky clay at the bottom. (The sticky clay is not permanent, so you will be able to disassemble the centerpiece if you wish.)

CREATE ARRANGEMENT

Create the arrangement by adding the flowers in one type at a time. Begin with the Delphiniums. Trim each stem to the desired height and bend a slight arc into each. Place them one by one from the back to the middle of the Styrofoam. (Cluster a few in the middle and add 1 or 2 to each side.) Next, add the Alliums in between the Delphiniums. (Their globe shape contrasts wonderfully with the delphinium spikes.) These 2 types of flowers create the top main layer of the arrangement. Next, add 2 clusters of arcing Lily of the Valley to each side, creating a level of flowers just above the bowl's edge. Complete the bottom level of the arrangement by adding in the saucer-shaped Hellebore blooms and the Fern fronds where there is empty space. The blooms will spill over the front and partially obscure the edge of the bowl to create a natural, luscious look.

Victorian Arrangement

Growing up, I went with my mother to many estate sales and flea markets, where we collected floral arrangements of all varieties: paper, silk, wax, and more. My favorites were from the Victorian era—tall arrangements that were traditionally placed on either side of a mantel, often under a glass dome or bell jar. I love things with a sense of history, and this Victorian-inspired arrangement is my modern take on this element of romantic décor.

PREPARE MATERIALS

This arrangement is approximately 30" tall x 14" wide (76 x 35.5 cm). To start, make 1 Campanula (page 72), 1 Bearded Iris with a single bud (page 80), 2 Fern fronds (page 162, assembled as shown on page 27), 3 Eden Roses and 2 buds (page 40), 10 Fluffy Poppies (page 44), 2 Lilies of the Valley (page 114), 1 Honeysuckle (page 110), 1 small Allium (page 32), 1 Charm Peony (page 36), 1 sprig of Coleus (page 122), 1 Plum Fruit Branch (page 118), and 2 Rhododendron leaf sprays (page 52). You will also need 18" (46 cm) lengths 18-gauge reinforcement wire, floral tape, floral sticky clay, Styrofoam, and a cylindrical vase or vessel that fits on your mantel.

CREATE ARRANGEMENT

Begin by creating the top cluster. Tape the Campanula and Bearded Iris with bud together, positioning them so that the blooms are facing the front. Place a Fern behind the 2 first blooms to create the main stem. Use 5 Fluffy Poppies to fill in spaces close to the main stem (and deeper in the arrangement).

Next, add the showier blooms farther out from the main stem so they are visible and have enough room so that they're not smashed: Add 1 Eden Rose at the top right of the arrangement and another to the right below the Campanula.

Next, add the 2 Eden Rose buds to right of the bloom. Fill the spaces below and to the right of the Eden Roses with 2 Fluffy Poppies. Add 2 Lilies of the Valley and 1 more Eden Rose in the center, then place the Honeysuckle to the left. Place the second Fern frond behind the 2 Lilies of the Valley. Add in 2 more Fluffy Poppies to fill in the empty spaces. Then attach a small Allium on the right, 1 Charm Peony in the center, and a Coleus sprig on the left. Finish with the Plum Branch on the left, the last Fluffy Poppy in the center, and the 2 Rhododendron sprays positioned at the right. Adjust the blooms and leaves as you go so that everything looks natural and has room to breathe. Finish each stem with reinforcement wires as needed, turn the arrangement over, and finish the stems with floral tape.

PREPARE VASE AND ARRANGE FLOWERS

Cut a piece of Styrofoam to fit tightly in the vase 1" (2.5 cm) below the lip of the bowl. If the Styrofoam is not tightly wedged in, secure it with a small piece or two of floral sticky clay. (The sticky clay is not permanent, so you will be able to disassemble the arrangement if you wish.) Insert the main stem into the foam, so that the blooms just peek out of the top of the vase.

PAGE 136

Peony Bouquet
PAGE 135

This Peony Bouquet is a very romantic, very feminine piece, especially since it's filled with the wildly fluffy Charm Peonies. This project is composed of all globe-shaped flowers that, when put together, create a cloudlike arrangement. It's perfect for a centerpiece for an event or a permanent arrangement for your home. When creating this arrangement, be sure to build from the center out, as the blooms don't fit quite as nicely together from the outside in.

PREPARE MATERIALS

This arrangement is approximately 18" tall x 24" long (46 x 61 cm) when completed. I used 7 assorted Charm Peonies (page 36) and 3 Peony buds (page 24), 6 Hydrangea clusters (page 48), and 8 Hydrangea leaves in green and painted paper (see page 17). You will also need scissors, Styrofoam sheet, 1 low bowl, floral sticky clay (optional), and wire cutters.

PREPARE BOWL

Cut a piece of Styrofoam to fit tightly in the bowl so that it sits 1" (2.5 cm) below the lip of the bowl. If the Styrofoam is not tightly wedged in, secure it with a small piece or two of floral sticky clay. (The sticky clay is not permanent, so you will be able to disassemble the arrangement if you wish.)

CREATE ARRANGEMENT

Trim each bloom to the desired height: the Hydrangeas should be slightly shorter than the Peonies. Start by adding 3 Charm Peonies to the center of the Styrofoam piece. Then, fill in the area behind and a bit below the Charm Peonies with 3 Hydrangea blooms and 4 Hydrangea leaves (I recess the Hydrangea blooms a level behind the Charm Peonies so that they are secondary to them). Next, add the secondary layer of 4 Charm Peonies around the perimeter of the arrangement, again filling in with the remaining 3 Hydrangea blooms and 4 Hydrangea leaves after. Finally, add the 3 Peony buds to the arrangement to break up the shape a bit and add interest to the arrangement.

Dutch Still-Life Centerpiece
PAGE 148

I've always loved the idea of incorporating as many stems in the book into a single arrangement as possible, and with this Dutch Still-Life Centerpiece, I think I've finally achieved this goal without going too over the top. True, this might be called "the kitchen sink" of arrangements, but it's absolutely gorgeous.

PREPARE MATERIALS

This arrangement is approximately 36" tall x 24" wide (91 x 61 cm). You will need 1 to 2 stems of each flower in this book. You will also need scissors, Styrofoam sheet, 1 bowl at least 12" (30.5 cm) wide by at least 3" (7.5 cm) deep, floral sticky clay (optional), and wire cutters.

PREPARE BOWL

Cut a piece of Styrofoam to fit tightly in the bowl so that it sits 1" (2.5 cm) below the lip of the dish. If the Styrofoam is not tightly wedged in, secure it with a small piece or two of floral sticky clay. (The sticky clay is not permanent, so you will be able to disassemble the arrangement if you wish.)

ARRANGE FLOWERS

Using wire cutters, trim the stems of the blooms. Insert them into the foam, creating interesting groupings with some stems closer to the foam and some higher. This creates "ins and outs" that will help your arrangement have a more natural look. I like to group blooms of similar shapes together in bundles of 2 and 3, but you should play around with the flowers and see what looks good to your eye.

TEMPLATES

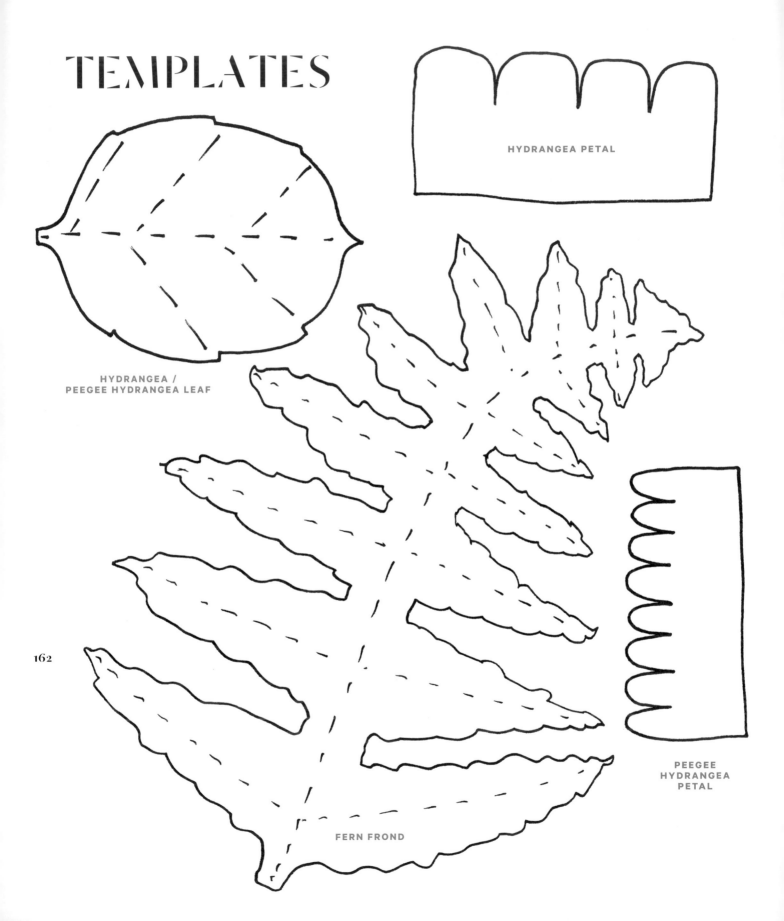

HYDRANGEA PETAL

HYDRANGEA /
PEEGEE HYDRANGEA LEAF

PEEGEE
HYDRANGEA
PETAL

162

FERN FROND

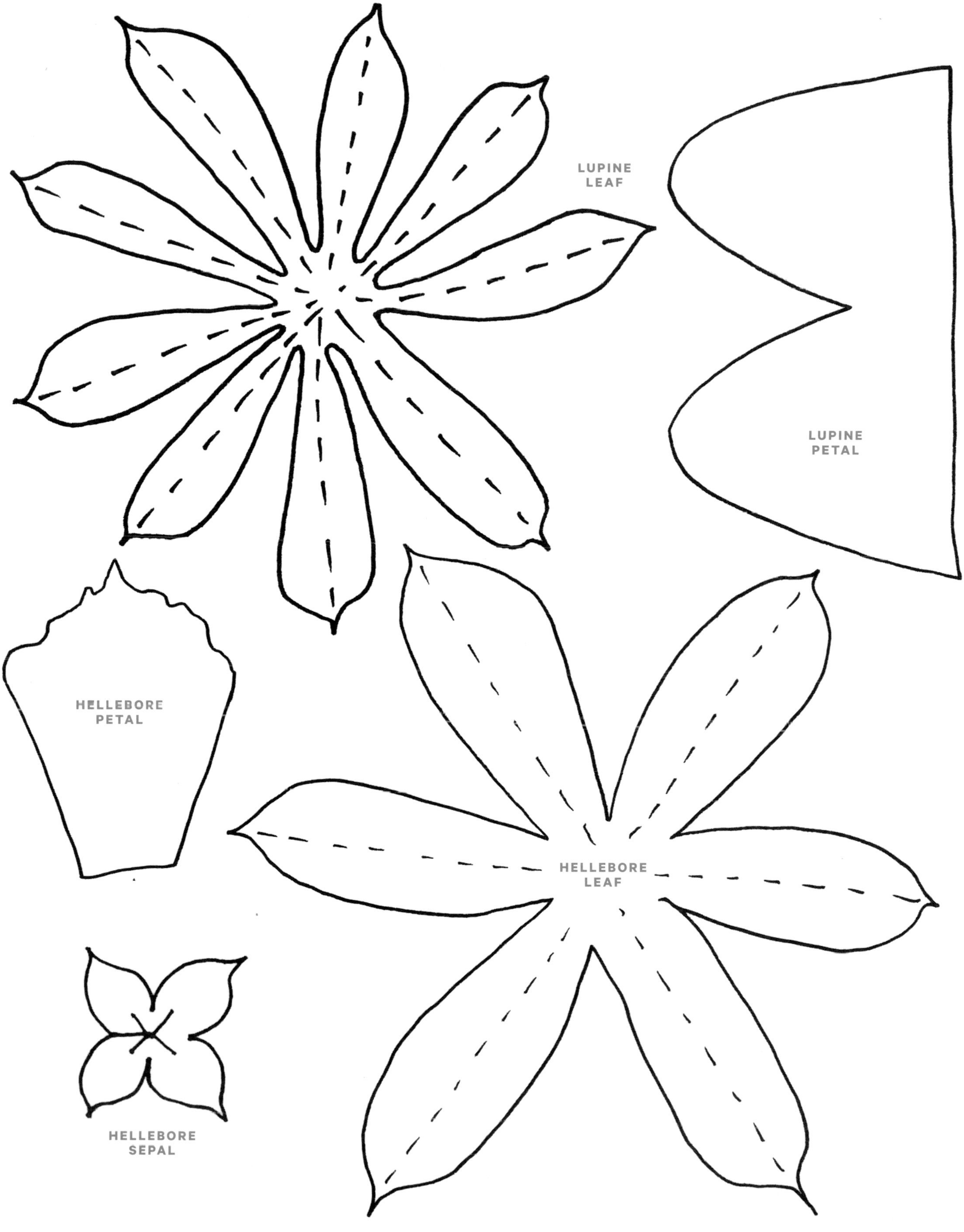

LUPINE
LEAF

LUPINE
PETAL

HELLEBORE
PETAL

HELLEBORE
LEAF

HELLEBORE
SEPAL

CORNFLOWER LEAF 1

CORNFLOWER LEAF 2

CORNFLOWER LEAF 3

CORNFLOWER PETAL

NASHI PETAL

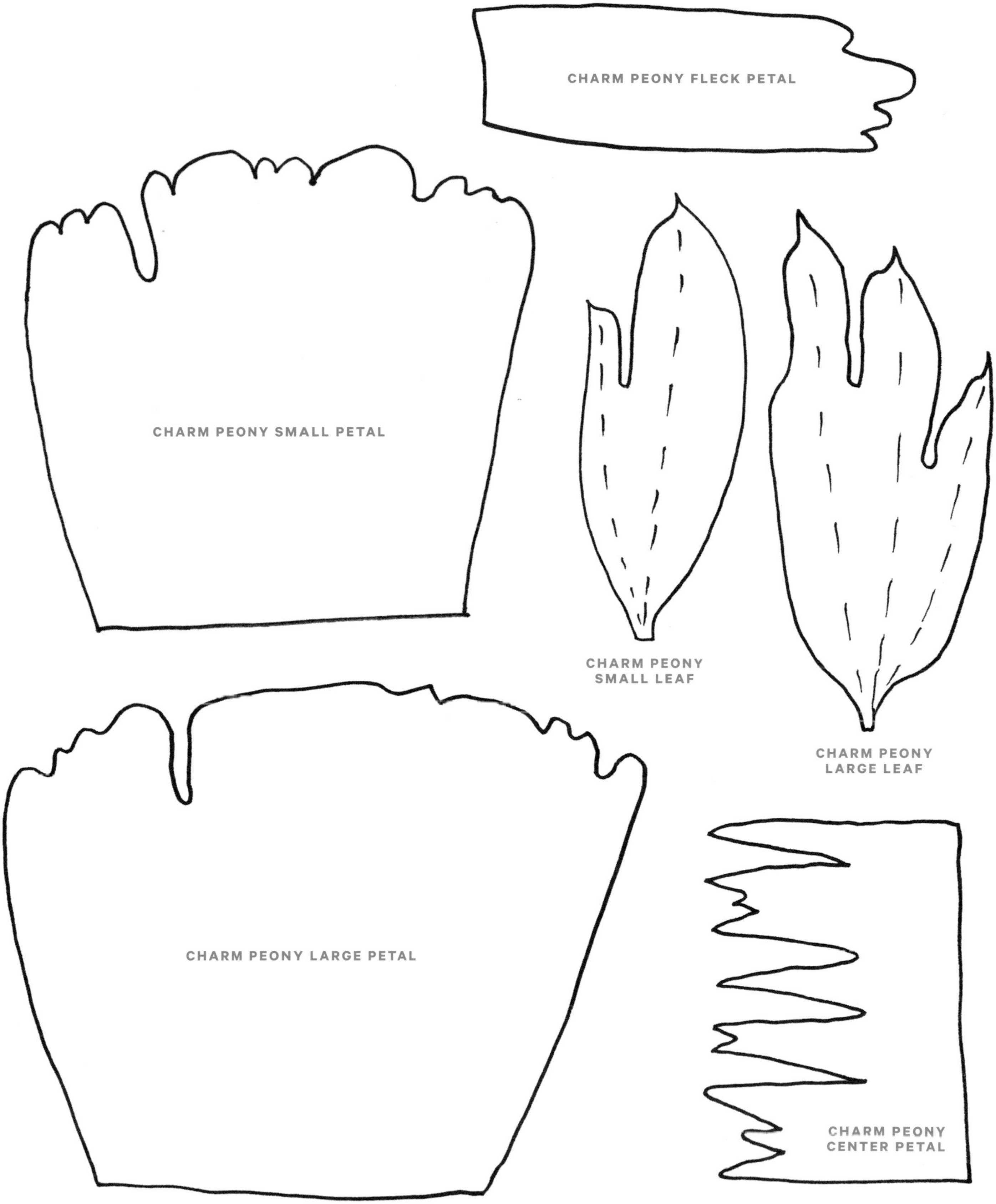

CHARM PEONY FLECK PETAL

CHARM PEONY SMALL PETAL

CHARM PEONY
SMALL LEAF

CHARM PEONY
LARGE LEAF

CHARM PEONY LARGE PETAL

CHARM PEONY
CENTER PETAL

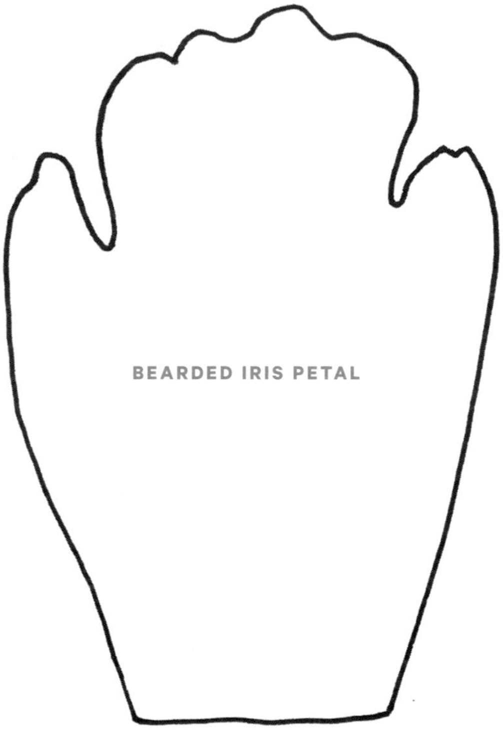

BEARDED IRIS PETAL

BEARDED IRIS
BUD LEAF CASING

BEARDED
IRIS FRILL

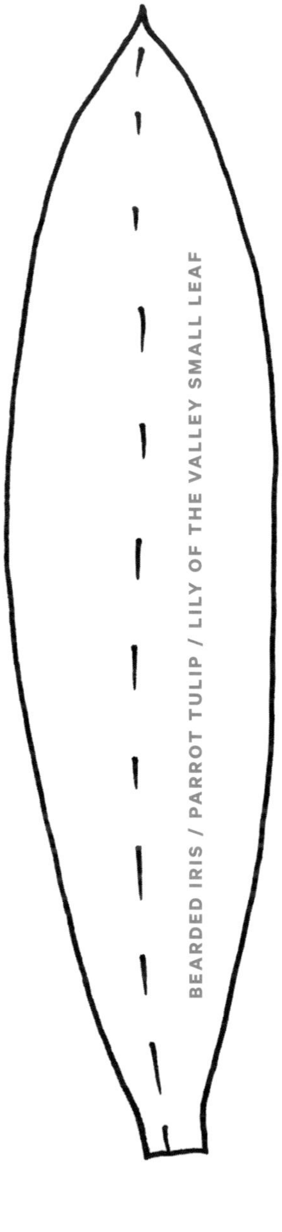

BEARDED IRIS / PARROT TULIP / LILY OF THE VALLEY SMALL LEAF

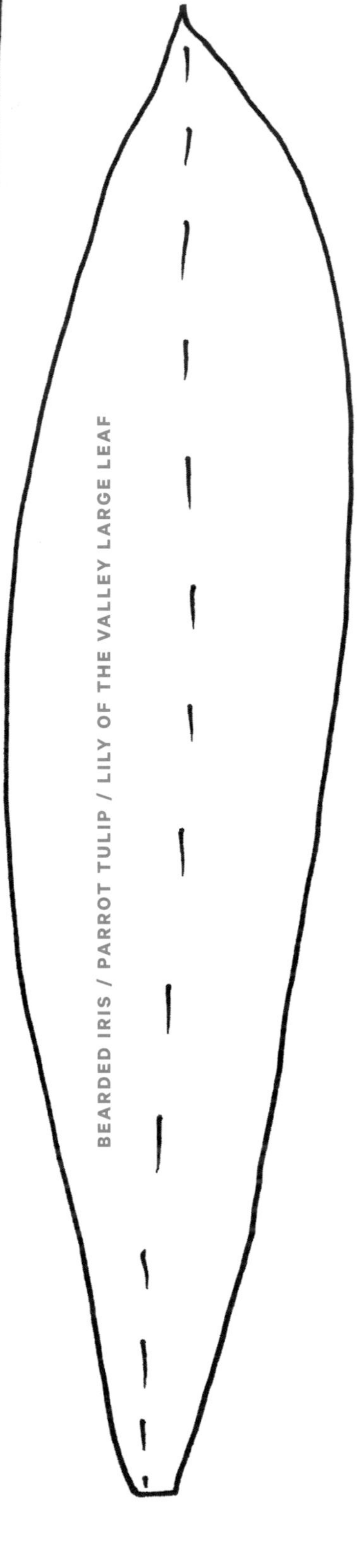

BEARDED IRIS / PARROT TULIP / LILY OF THE VALLEY LARGE LEAF

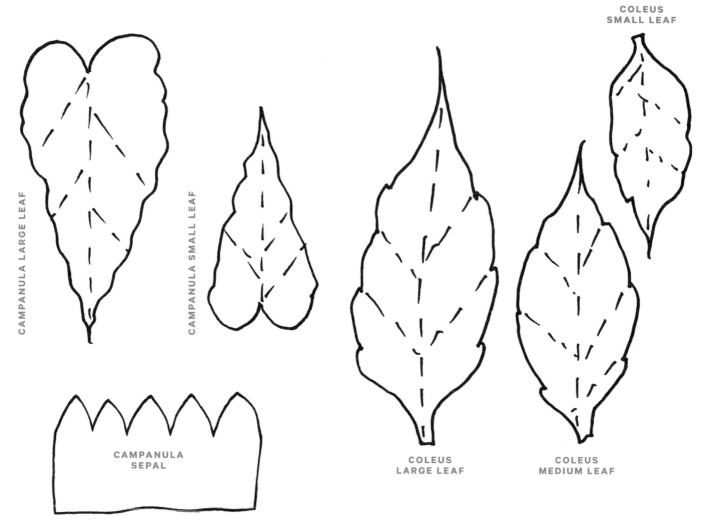

COLEUS
SMALL LEAF

CAMPANULA LARGE LEAF

CAMPANULA SMALL LEAF

CAMPANULA
SEPAL

COLEUS
LARGE LEAF

COLEUS
MEDIUM LEAF

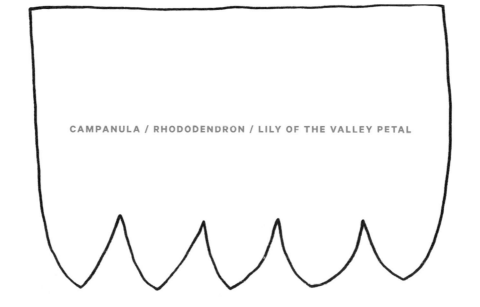

CAMPANULA / RHODODENDRON / LILY OF THE VALLEY PETAL

THE EXQUISITE BOOK OF
PAPER FLOWER TRANSFORMATIONS

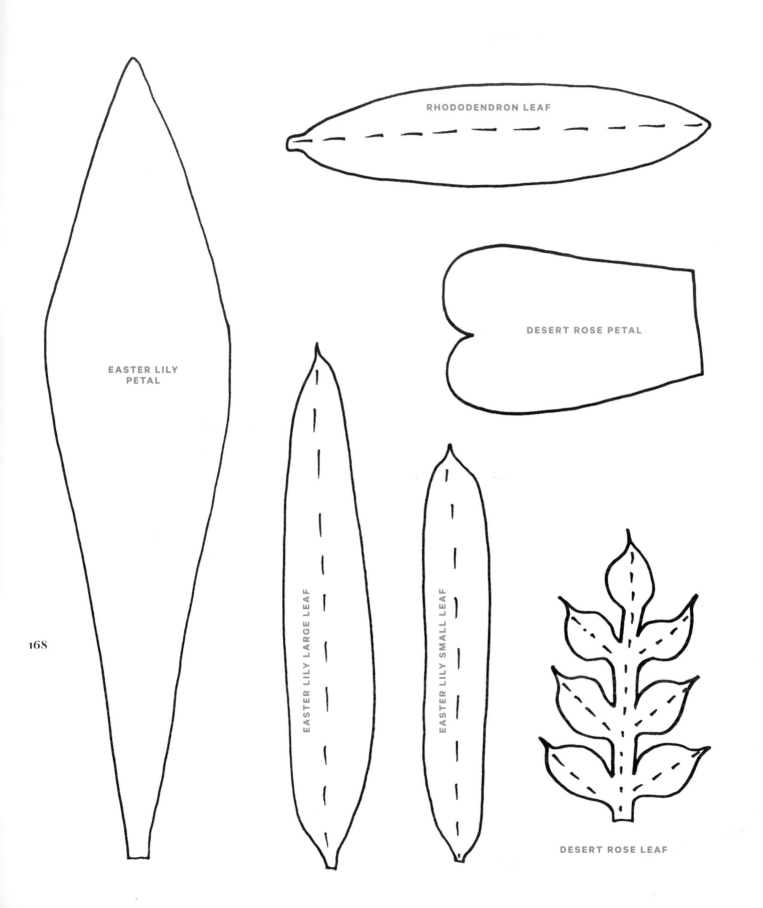

RHODODENDRON LEAF

DESERT ROSE PETAL

EASTER LILY
PETAL

EASTER LILY LARGE LEAF

EASTER LILY SMALL LEAF

DESERT ROSE LEAF

EDEN ROSE SMALL PETAL

ALLIUM PETAL

EDEN ROSE MEDIUM PETAL

EDEN ROSE SMALL LEAF

EDEN ROSE LARGE LEAF

EDEN ROSE LARGE PETAL

PARROT TULIP PETAL

DELPHINIUM LEAF

DELPHINIUM LARGE PETAL

DELPHINIUM SMALL PETAL

170

HONEYSUCKLE SMALL LEAF

HONEYSUCKLE LARGE LEAF

HONEYSUCKLE
PETAL

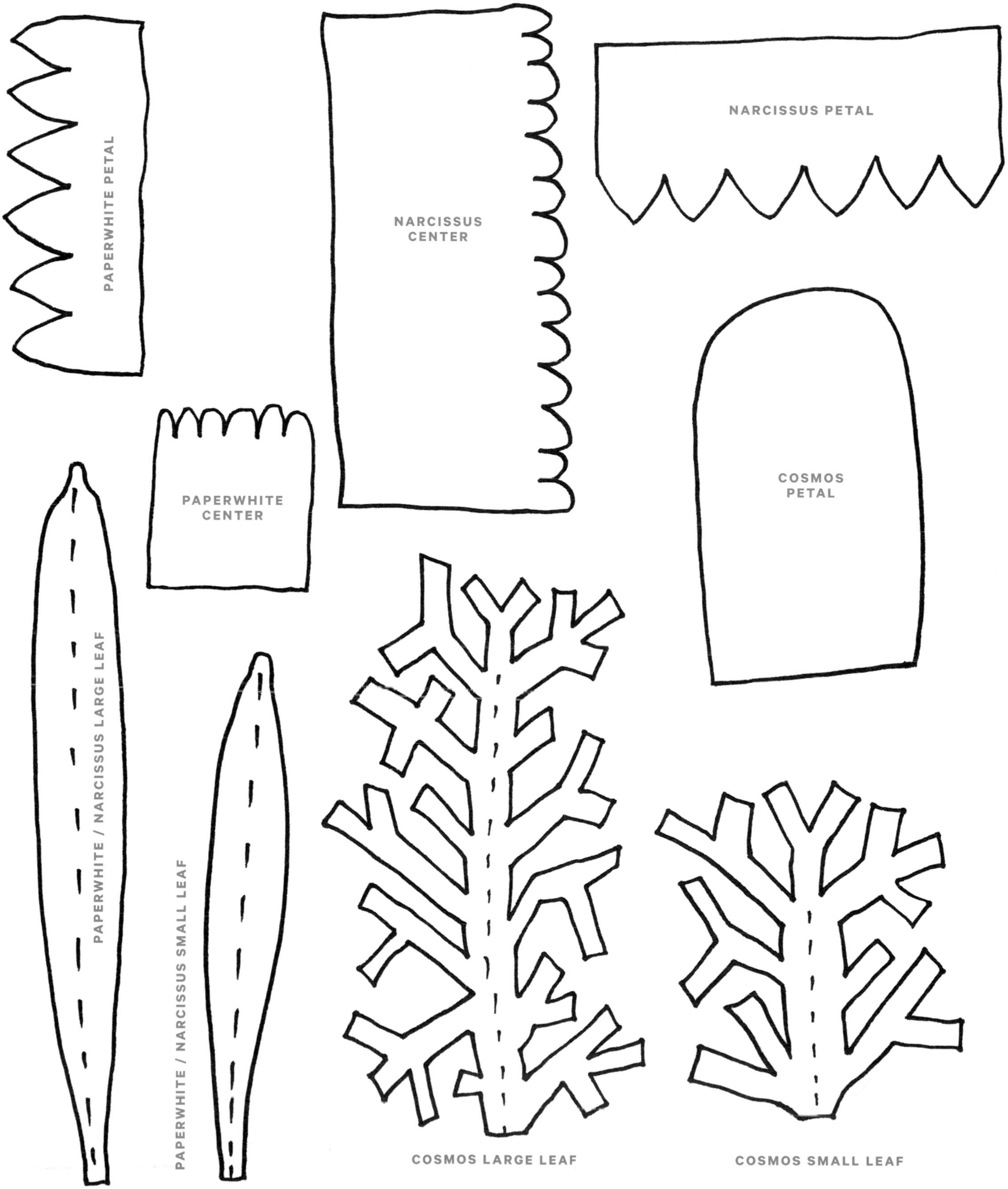

PAPERWHITE PETAL

NARCISSUS CENTER

NARCISSUS PETAL

COSMOS PETAL

PAPERWHITE CENTER

PAPERWHITE / NARCISSUS LARGE LEAF

PAPERWHITE / NARCISSUS SMALL LEAF

COSMOS LARGE LEAF

COSMOS SMALL LEAF

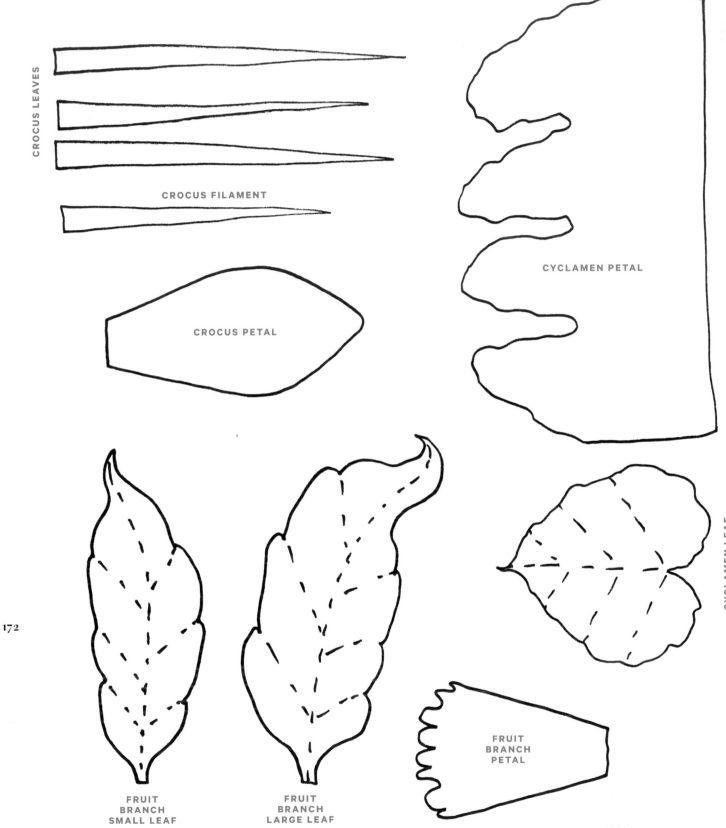

CROCUS LEAVES

CROCUS FILAMENT

CROCUS PETAL

CYCLAMEN PETAL

CYCLAMEN LEAF

172

FRUIT
BRANCH
SMALL LEAF

FRUIT
BRANCH
LARGE LEAF

FRUIT
BRANCH
PETAL

RESOURCES

The materials and tools used in the projects in this book are generally available at arts and crafts supply stores nationwide. If you cannot find what you are looking for locally, try these online sources.

———

A.C. MOORE
www.acmoore.com

DHARMA TRADING CO.
www.dharmatrading.com

DICK BLICK ART MATERIALS
www.dickblick.com

JO-ANN FABRIC AND CRAFTS
www.joann.com

MICHAEL'S STORES
www.michaels.com

SAVE-ON-CRAFTS
www.save-on-crafts.com

UTRECHT
www.utrechtart.com

Additional Sources

Doublette and Fine Crepe Paper
CASTLE IN THE AIR
www.castleintheair.biz

Fringing Shears
BELL'OCHIO
www.bellochio.com

Floral Tape
JAMALI FLORAL AND GARDEN SUPPLY
www.jamaligarden.com

Mini Cotton Swabs
MUJI
www.muji.com/us

Printed Cotton Twine
PURL SOHO
www.purlsoho.com

Tissue Paper
BAGS & BOWS
www.bagsandbowsonline.com
NASHVILLE WRAPS
www.nashvillewraps.com

Vintage Fruit
TAIL OF THE YAK TRADING CO
510-841-9891

Vintage Stamens
TINSEL TRADING
www.tinseltrading.com

ACKNOWLEDGMENTS

Thanks to my agent, Judy Linden at Stonesong,
who's always had my back.

Thanks to my publishing team at Abrams,
especially my awesome editor,
Cristina Garces, who kept me on track.

Many, many thanks to Erica Sanders-Foege
for translating my ideas into English and
guiding me though this incredible process.

Thanks to Jaspal Riyait for design awesomeness!

Kate Mathis, thanks for adding a ray of sunlight
to every beautiful picture you take.

My thanks to Joie Meffert and Marta Portillo,
whom I depend upon for all my help and support.

Thank you Mom and Dad, for always valuing
creativity and encouraging me to follow my dreams.

And saving the best for last, thank you
Dante, Mick, and Dan . . . all my love.

Props and materials used in the photographs in this book were provided by:

—

ABC CARPET AND HOME
www.abchome.com

ASTIER DE VILLATTE
www.astierdevillatte.com

BIRD + BOWER
www.birdandbower.com

JOHN DERIAN COMPANY INC.
www.johnderian.com

MUD AUSTRALIA
www.mudaustralia.com

PAPER TRAIL
www.papertrailrhinebeck.com

PARCEL
www.shopparcel.com

PROP HAUS
www.prophaus.com

XENOMANIA
www.xeno-mania.com

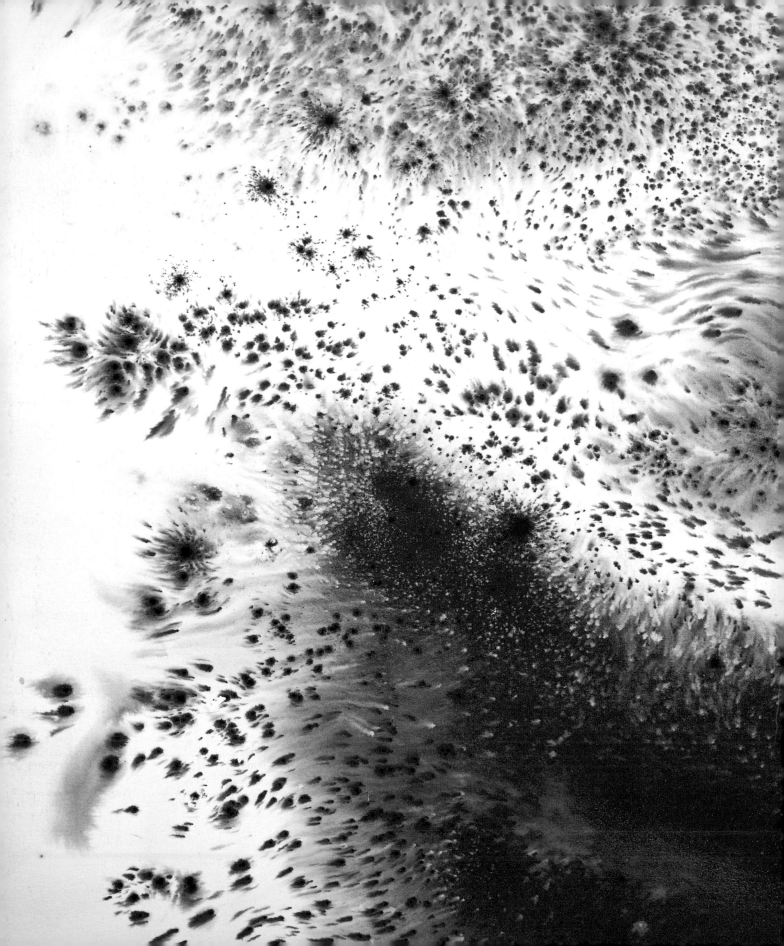